GCSE OCR 21st Century
Core Science
Foundation — the Basics
The Workbook

This book is for anyone doing **GCSE OCR 21st Century Core Science** at foundation level, with a predicted grade of D or below.
(If you're not sure what your predicted grade is, your teacher will be able to tell you.)

It's full of **useful practice questions** to help you **get to grips with** the essential science you'll need for the exams.

And of course, there are some daft bits to make the whole thing vaguely entertaining for you.

What CGP is all about

Our sole aim here at CGP is to produce the highest quality books — carefully written, immaculately presented and dangerously close to being funny.

Then we work our socks off to get them out to you — at the cheapest possible prices.

Contents

MODULE B1 — YOU AND YOUR GENES

Genes, Chromosomes and DNA 1
Genes and Variation 2
Inheritance and Genetic Diagrams.. 4
Genetic Diagrams and Sex Chromosomes............................ 6
Genetic Disorders... 7
Genetic Testing 8
Clones 9
Stem Cells.. 10
Mixed Questions — Module B1 11

MODULE B2 — KEEPING HEALTHY

Microorganisms and Disease 13
The Immune System 14
Vaccination..15
Antibiotics 16
Drug Trials 18
The Circulatory System 19
Heart Rate and Blood Pressure 20
Heart Disease...21
Homeostasis and The Kidneys 22
Controlling Water Content 23
Mixed Questions — Module B2 24

MODULE B3 — LIFE ON EARTH

Adaptation and Variation 25
Natural Selection and Selective Breeding.......................... 26
Evolution 27
Biodiversity and Classification.. 29
Energy in an Ecosystem 30
Interactions Between Organisms 32
The Carbon Cycle.. 34
The Nitrogen Cycle... 35
Measuring Environmental Change....................................... 36
Sustainability 37
Mixed Questions — Module B3.. 39

MODULE C1 — AIR QUALITY

How the Air was Made... 40
The Air Today 41
Chemical Reactions 42
Fuels 44
Air Pollution — Carbon 45
Air Pollution — Sulfur and Nitrogen.................................... 46
Reducing Pollution 48
Mixed Questions — Module C1.. 50

MODULE C2 — MATERIAL CHOICES

Natural and Synthetic Materials 52
Materials and Properties 53
Materials, Properties and Uses 54
Crude Oil 55
Uses of Crude Oil 56
Polymerisation.. 57
Structure and Properties of Polymers 58
Nanotechnology... 60
Mixed Questions — Module C2.. 61

Module C3 — Chemicals in Our Lives

Tectonic Plates...63
Resources in the Earth's Crust...64
Salt..65
Salt in the Food Industry..66
Electrolysis of Salt Solution..67
Chlorination 68
Alkalis...69
Impacts of Chemical Production 70
Life Cycle Assessments..71
Mixed Questions — Module C3...73

Module P1 — The Earth in the Universe

The Solar System 75
Beyond the Solar System 76
Looking Into Space 77
The Life of the Universe...78
The Changing Earth 79
Wegener's Theory of Continental Drift.................................80
The Structure of the Earth 82
Seismic Waves 83
Waves — The Basics 84
Mixed Questions — Module P1 86

Module P2 — Radiation and Life

Electromagnetic Radiation 88
Electromagnetic Radiation and Energy.................................89
Ionising Radiation 90
Microwaves 92
Electromagnetic Radiation and the Atmosphere...................93
The Carbon Cycle..94
Global Warming and Climate Change..................................95
Electromagnetic Waves and Communication 96
Analogue and Digital Signals 97
Mixed Questions — Module P2..98

Module P3 — Sustainable Energy

Electrical Energy 100
Efficiency..103
Sankey Diagrams 105
Saving Energy 106
Energy Sources and Power Stations...................................107
Nuclear Energy..108
Wind and Solar Energy 109
Wave and Tidal Energy 110
Biofuels and Geothermal Energy.......................................111
Hydroelectricity and Reliable Fuel Supplies 112
Comparing Energy Resources 113
Generators and the National Grid......................................114
Mixed Questions — Module P3..115

Published by CGP

Editors:
Luke Antieul, Katie Braid, Katherine Craig, Emma Elder, Ben Fletcher, Edmund Robinson, Rachael Rogers, Helen Ronan, Hayley Thompson, Jane Towle.

Contributors:
Mark A Edwards, Paddy Gannon.

ISBN: 978 1 84762 720 9

With thanks to Rosie McCurrie and Dawn Wright for the proofreading.
With thanks to Jeremy Cooper, Janet Cruse-Sawyer and Ian Francis for the reviewing.
With thanks to Jan Greenway, Laura Jakubowski and Laura Stoney for the copyright research.

Data on page 49 courtesy of Haynes Publishing.

Groovy website: www.cgpbooks.co.uk

Printed by Elanders Ltd, Newcastle upon Tyne.
Jolly bits of clipart from CorelDRAW®

Based on the classic CGP style created by Richard Parsons.

Psst... photocopying this Workbook isn't allowed, even if you've got a CLA licence. Luckily, it's dead cheap, easy and quick to order more copies from CGP — just call us on 0870 750 1242. Phew!
Text, design, layout and original illustrations © Coordination Group Publications Ltd. (CGP) 2011
All rights reserved.

Module B1 — You and Your Genes

Genes, Chromosomes and DNA

Q1 Complete the sentences using the words below.

> gene   protein   chromosome   nucleus

a) Each .... is a short bit of DNA.

b) Each .... is one very long bit of DNA.

c) A gene tells a cell how to make a ....

d) Chromosomes are found in a cell's ....

Q2 Draw lines to match up the types of protein with the examples.

TYPE OF PROTEIN   EXAMPLE

functional protein   collagen

structural protein   enzymes

Q3 Which of these is **true**? Tick **one** box.

☐ Eye colour is controlled by just one gene.

☐ Eye colour is controlled by many genes.

☐ Eye colour is controlled by the environment.

☐ Eye colour is controlled by the environment and just one gene.

Q4 Circle the correct words in the sentences below.

All / Some characteristics are controlled by genes.

Weight is controlled by an organism's **genes alone / genes and environment**.

Scars are controlled by an organism's **environment / genes**.

Dimples are controlled by an organism's **environment / genes**.

Genes and Variation

Q1 Draw lines to complete the sentences.

Male sex cells are called...   fertilised eggs.

Female sex cells are called...   sperm.

Male and female sex cells join together to make...   eggs.

Q2 Are the following sentences **true** or **false**? Circle the answers.

a) The chromosomes in a human **skin** cell are found in pairs.

true   false

b) The chromosomes in a human **sex** cell are found in pairs.

true   false

Q3 Circle the right words in the paragraph below.

Children get **all / half** of their chromosomes from their mum.

Children get **half / none** of their chromosomes from their dad.

This is why children look **a bit like / identical to** both of their parents.

Q4 Add the labels in the boxes to the diagram.

sex cell   body cell

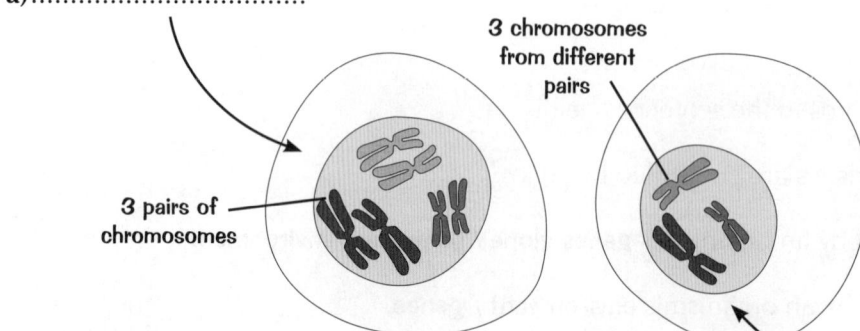

a) ....

3 pairs of chromosomes

3 chromosomes from different pairs

b) ....

Module B1 — You and Your Genes

Genes and Variation

Q5 The diagram below shows a **pair** of human **chromosomes**. The gene for ear lobes is marked on chromosome B.

a) Where would you find the gene for ear lobes on **chromosome A?**
Circle the diagram below that shows the answer.

b) Chromosome A came from the **mother**. Where must chromosome B have come from?

....

c) What are different versions of the same gene called?

....

Q6 The picture below shows two **sisters**. They have the **same parents**.

Tick the boxes to show whether the statements are **true** or **false**.

		True	False
a)	The sisters look different because of sexual reproduction.	☐	☐
b)	The sisters come from different sex cells.	☐	☐
c)	Different sex cells contain the same alleles.	☐	☐

Module B1 — You and Your Genes

Inheritance and Genetic Diagrams

Q1 You have **two** alleles for each gene.

a) If both alleles are **dominant**, what characteristic will be shown? Circle the answer.

the recessive characteristic   the dominant characteristic

b) If both alleles are **recessive**, what characteristic will be shown? Circle the answer.

the recessive characteristic   the dominant characteristic

c) What characteristic will be shown if one allele is **recessive** and one allele is **dominant**? Circle the answer.

the recessive characteristic   the dominant characteristic

Q2 In butter plants the allele for **yellow flowers** (**Y**) is **dominant**. The allele for **white flowers** (**y**) is **recessive**.

Two plants reproduce. Complete the diagram to show the alleles the baby plants could inherit.

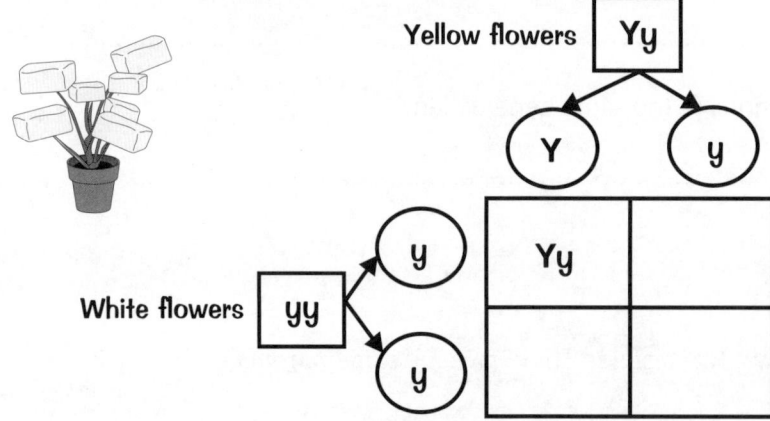

Q3 The **R** allele for being able to **roll your tongue** is **dominant**. The **r** allele for **not** being able to roll your tongue is **recessive**.

Circle the words to complete the sentences.

Not being able to roll your tongue is caused by a **recessive** / **dominant** allele.

It will only show up when there **is one copy** / **are two copies** of the allele.

Sandeep can't roll his tongue.

This means that Sandeep must have the alleles **rr** / **Rr**.

Module B1 — You and Your Genes

Inheritance and Genetic Diagrams

Q4 In cats the allele for black fur (**B**) is **dominant**. The allele for brown fur (**b**) is **recessive**.

a) Two cats have kittens. Complete the Punnett square to show the alleles the kittens could get.

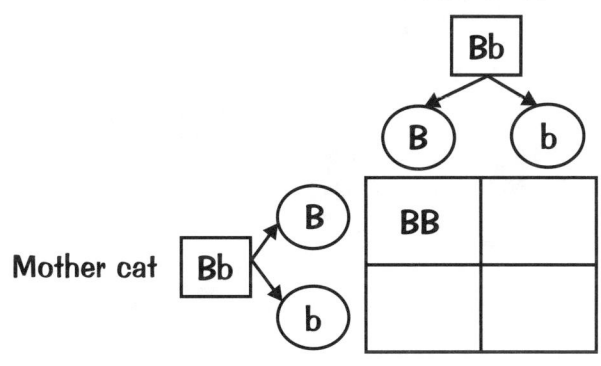

b) What colour fur will kittens with the following alleles have?

BB .... Bb .... bb ....

Q5 The allele for **dimples** (**D**) is **dominant**. The allele for **no dimples** (**d**) is **recessive**.

a) Jody and Mike are having a baby.
Complete the Punnett square to show the genes the baby could inherit.

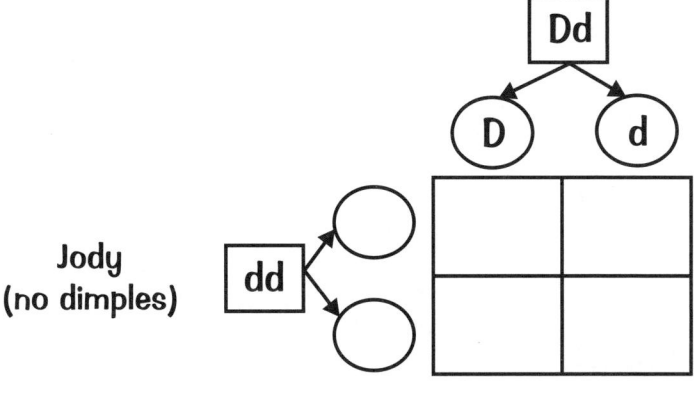

b) Will children with the following alleles have dimples? Write '**yes**' or '**no**'.

Dd .... dd ....

c) What is the chance of the baby having dimples? Circle the answer.

| 1 in 4 | 1 in 2 | 3 in 4 |

Module B1 — You and Your Genes

Genetic Diagrams and Sex Chromosomes

Q1 The **family tree** below shows a family with a gene for x-ray vision.

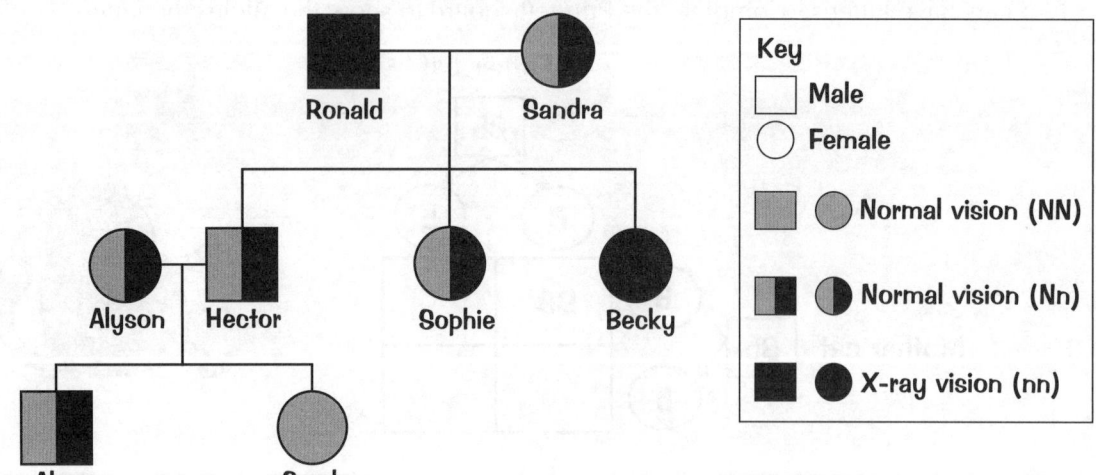

a) What alleles does **Hector** have? Circle your answer.

| NN | Nn | nn |

Use the key to help you answer the questions.

b) Who has **x-ray vision**? Circle the **two** correct answers.

| Sarah | Becky | Alex | Ronald |

Q2 Use the words to fill in the gaps in the passage below.

 Y   sex

 boys   X

Everybody has one pair chromosomes that decide whether you're a boy or girl.

These chromosomes are called the …................. chromosomes.

The …................. chromosome is found in boys and girls.

But the …................. chromosome is only found in boys.

Module B1 — You and Your Genes

Genetic Disorders

Q1 **Huntington's disease** is caused by a **faulty** allele.

a) Is the allele that causes Huntington's disease **dominant** or **recessive**? Circle the answer.

> dominant   recessive

b) What are the **symptoms** of Huntington's disease? Tick **three** answers.

☐ tremors   ☐ clumsiness   ☐ finding it hard to breathe

☐ thick mucus   ☐ memory loss

c) Huntington's disease is a **late onset disease**. What does this mean?
Circle the right words to complete the answer.

> People with Huntington's disease only get symptoms late **in their lives / each day**.

Q2 Libby has **cystic fibrosis**.

a) Is cystic fibrosis caused by a **dominant** or a **recessive** allele?

....

b) Write down two symptoms of cystic fibrosis that Libby might have.

1. ....

2. ....

c) Libby's sister is a **carrier** of cystic fibrosis. What is a carrier?
Tick the answer.

Someone with two copies of the dominant allele. ☐

Someone with only one copy of the recessive allele. ☐

Someone with two copies of the recessive allele. ☐

Module B1 — You and Your Genes

Genetic Testing

Q1 What is genetic testing? Tick the answer.

☐ It's where you test each gene to see if it works.

☐ It's where you look at a person's DNA to see what alleles they have.

☐ It's where you measure the length of a person's DNA.

Q2 If a woman has problems getting pregnant, doctors can put embryos inside her. The embryos have **genetic tests** first.

a) Why do the embryos have genetic tests? Tick the answer.

| To see how big the embryos will grow. ☐ | So that only healthy embryos are used. ☐ | To make sure only embryos with green eyes are used. ☐ |

b) It isn't always safe to carry out genetic tests during pregnancy. Explain why.

....

Q3 People can be genetically tested **before** being **given drugs**. Why does this happen? Tick **two** correct answers.

To make sure the drug isn't illegal. ☐

To tell the doctor if the drug will work well. ☐

To see if the person will have a dangerous reaction to the drug. ☐

To check the drug isn't too expensive. ☐

Q4 Draw lines between the boxes to complete the sentences.

| A false positive is when... | ...a healthy person is told that they have a genetic disorder. |

| A false negative is when... | ...a person with a genetic disorder is told that they are fit and well. |

Q5 Sam has had a **genetic test**. It shows he has a genetic disorder and will get ill in the future. His **insurance company** has seen the results of the test. What **problem** might this cause?

....

Module B1 — You and Your Genes

Clones

Q1 Which of these is **true**? Circle **one** answer.

- Clones have exactly the same genes as each other.
- Clones are a type of plant.
- Clones have slightly different genes to each other.

Q2 Tick the boxes to show whether the statements are **true** or **false**.

		True	False
a)	Bacteria can reproduce by asexual reproduction.	☐	☐
b)	All animals reproduce by asexual reproduction.	☐	☐
c)	There are two parents in asexual reproduction.	☐	☐

Q3 Plants can reproduce **asexually**.

How can they do this? Write down two ways.

1. ....
2. ....

Q4 Fred and Bob are **identical twins**.

a) How are identical twins made? Circle the correct words to complete the sentences.

> Identical twins are **clones** / **alleles**.
>
> They are made when **a specialised stem cell** / **an embryo** splits into two.

b) Fred is taller than Bob. Why are the twins different? Circle the answer below.

genes   the environment   recessive alleles

Module B1 — You and Your Genes

Stem Cells

Q1 Which of these are **true**? Tick **two** boxes.

- Most cells in your body are specialised. ☐
- Specialised cells can do any task. ☐
- Unspecialised cells are called stem cells. ☐
- Cells don't become specialised until you're an adult. ☐

Q2 Complete the passage below using the words in the box.

| embryos | adults | any type | many but not all types |

Embryonic stem cells are found in ....

They can turn into .... of cell.

Adult stem cells are found in ....

They can turn into .... of cell.

Q3 Sue and Pete are talking about uses of stem cells.
Only **one** of them is **right**.

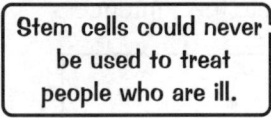

Sue: Stem cells could never be used to treat people who are ill.

Pete: Stem cells could be used to treat ill people. They could replace damaged cells.

Who is **right**, Sue or Pete?

....

Module B1 — You and Your Genes

Mixed Questions — Module B1

Q1 How are **clones** made? Circle **two** answers.

- when cells become specialised
- by asexual reproduction
- when an embryo splits in two
- by making structural proteins

Q2 The pictures below show the chromosomes of two people.

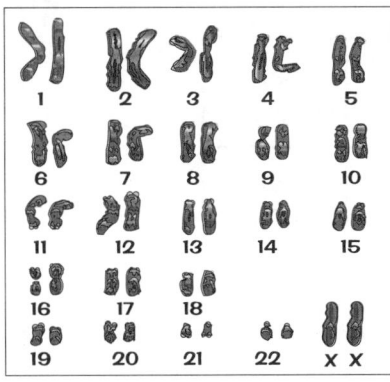
Person A

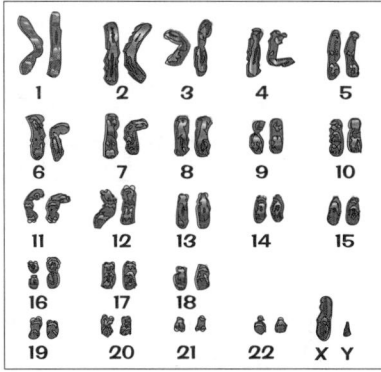
Person B

a) Which person is **female**? ....

b) How can you tell? ....

Q3 A genetic disorder is caused by a **dominant** allele (**T**).

a) The **Punnett square** shows a cross between two people with the alleles **Tt**. Fill it in.

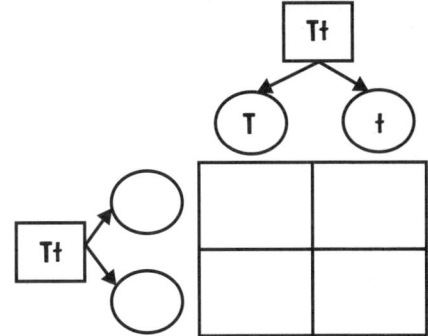

b) Will a child with the following alleles have the disorder? Write 'yes' or 'no'.

TT .... Tt .... tt ....

c) What is the chance of a child of this cross having the alleles **Tt** or **tt**? Circle your answer.

Add together the chance of a child having the alleles TT and Tt.

　　25%　　　　50%　　　　75%　　　　100%

d) What is the chance of a child of this cross having the disorder? Circle your answer.

　　25%　　　　50%　　　　75%　　　　100%

Module B1 — You and Your Genes

Mixed Questions — Module B1

Q4 A **genetic disease** is caused by a **recessive** allele (**a**).

The Punnett square shows a cross between Sean and Jenny.

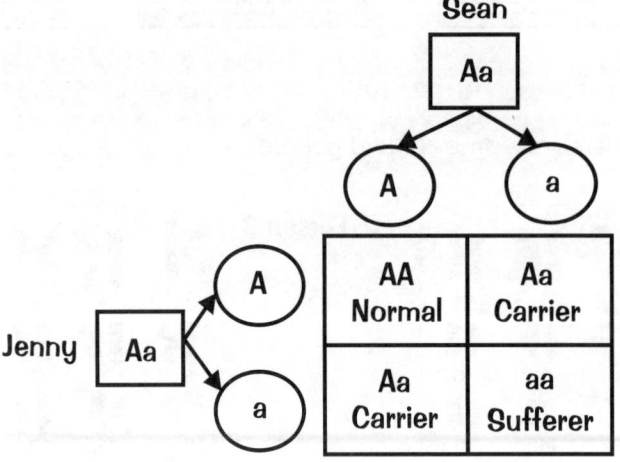

a) If Sean and Jenny have a child, what is the **chance** that the child will be a **carrier**? Circle the answer.

0%   25%   50%   75%   100%

b) Jenny has had a genetic test. She's found out that she's a carrier. She's been asking herself questions like the one below:

Suggest **one** other question Jenny might ask.

....

....

c) Jenny gets pregnant. A genetic test is carried out on the fetus. It's found to have the alleles **aa**. Circle the box below that describes the fetus.

normal   a carrier   a sufferer

Module B1 — You and Your Genes

Module B2 — Keeping Healthy

Microorganisms and Disease

Q1 Circle the right words in the sentences below.

> Microorganisms are things like bacteria and **viruses** / **rashes**.
>
> Some microorganisms cause **infectious diseases** / **antibiotics**. These often have symptoms.
>
> Microorganisms cause symptoms by **copying** / **damaging** your cells.
>
> They also cause symptoms by making **toxins** / **antigens**.

Q2 Bacteria **copy** themselves **quickly** inside the human body. Circle **three** reasons why.

- It's warm.
- It's dark.
- It's moist.
- There's food.
- There's lots of space.

Q3 A bacteria copies itself **once** every **15 minutes**. One bacteria is left for **30 minutes**.

a) How many bacteria are there after **15 minutes**? Circle the answer.

    2   4   8   16

b) How many bacteria are there after **30 minutes**? Circle the answer.

    2   4   8   16

Q4 A bacteria copies itself **once** every **10 minutes**. **Two bacteria** are left for **20 minutes**.

a) How many times will the bacteria copy themselves in 20 minutes? Tick the answer.

- [ ] once
- [ ] twice
- [ ] three times

b) How many bacteria will there be after 20 minutes? Circle the answer.

    2   4   8

The Immune System

Q1 What does your **immune system** do? Tick the answer.

It stops microorganisms getting out of your body. ☐

It kills microorganisms that get into your body. ☐

It helps microorganisms copy themselves inside your body. ☐

Q2 Circle the right words to complete the sentences.

> White blood cells can make **antibodies** / **antigens** to kill the microorganisms.
>
> They can also **engulf** / **inject** the microorganisms. Then they **digest** / **poison** them.

Q3 What is an **antigen**? Underline the answer.

A chemical that causes disease.   A chemical on the surface of a microorganism.   A chemical that destroys bacteria.

Q4 Are these sentences **true** or **false**? Tick the boxes.

		True	False
a)	Red blood cells detect the antigens on microorganisms.	☐	☐
b)	Antibodies are made by white blood cells.	☐	☐
c)	Different microorganisms have the same antigens.	☐	☐
d)	Different antibodies are needed to kill different microorganisms.	☐	☐

Q5 **Memory cells** stop you from getting a disease for a second time.

a) What are memory cells? Circle the answer.

special brain cells   special red blood cells   special white blood cells

b) How do memory cells stop you getting a disease for a second time? Tick the answer.

☐ They remember how to make the right antibodies.

☐ They remember how to digest the right microorganisms.

☐ They remember how to make the right poison for the microorganisms.

Module B2 — Keeping Healthy

Vaccination

Q1 What is a **vaccination**? Tick the right box.

☐ It's where you inject someone with dead microorganisms.

☐ It's where you inject someone with antibodies.

Q2 **Vaccinations** aren't risk-free for everyone.

a) Tick the box next to the statement that is **true**.

Vaccinations can cause side effects. ☐

People never have side effects when they take drugs. ☐

Side effects are the same in everyone. ☐

b) Why do some people react differently to vaccinations? Circle the answer.

because of differences in their eye colour   because of differences in their blood type   because of differences in their genes

Q3 Why do white blood cells make antibodies to attack **dead microorganisms**? Tick the answer.

☐ White blood cells only make the antibodies by chance.

☐ White blood cells never stop making antibodies.

☐ Dead microorganisms have the same antigens as living microorganisms.

☐ Microorganisms cause disease whether they are alive or dead.

Q4 Circle the right words in the sentences below.

After vaccination, some white blood cells become **vaccine cells / memory cells**.

They remember how to make the **antigens / antibodies**.

So when a live microorganism turns up, they can make **antigens / antibodies** really quickly.

This means you **get sick faster / don't get sick**.

Module B2 — Keeping Healthy

Antibiotics

Q1 What is an **antibiotic**? Underline your answer.

> A chemical that can kill viruses.
>
> A chemical on the surface of microorganisms.
>
> A chemical that can kill bacteria.
>
> A chemical made by the body to kill microorganisms.

Q2 A **new antibiotic** was discovered in 1970. It's very good at dealing with **disease X**. The graph shows the number of deaths from disease X since 1960.

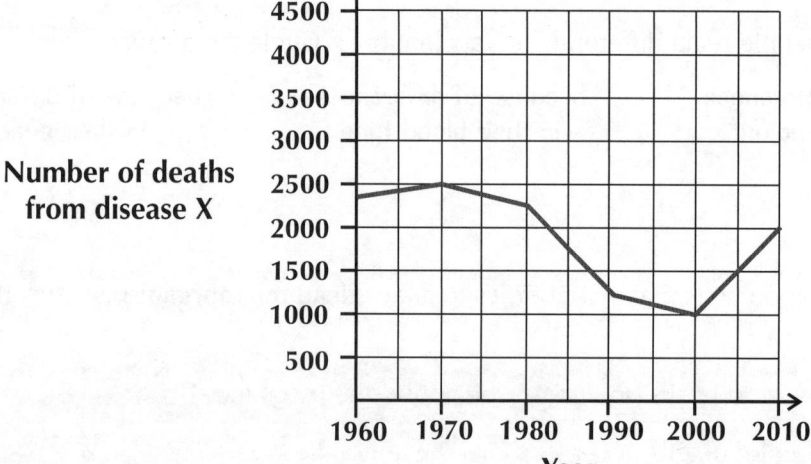

a) How many people died from disease X in **1970**? Circle the answer.

| 10 | 25 | 1000 | 2500 |

b) How many people died from disease X in **2000**? Circle the answer.

| 10 | 25 | 1000 | 2500 |

c) Deaths suddenly **increased** between 2000 and 2010. What could have caused this? Tick the answer.

> A virus might have started to cause the disease. ☐
>
> The bacteria that cause disease X might have become resistant to the antibiotic. ☐

Module B2 — Keeping Healthy

Antibiotics

Q3 a) Bacteria can become **resistant to antibiotics**. What does this mean? Circle the answer.

> **Antibiotics don't affect them.**   **Antibiotics take longer to affect them.**

b) Circle the correct words to complete the passage.

> Doctors can make it harder for bacteria to become resistant. They can do this by giving people antibiotics **only when they need them / for all infections**.

Q4 Gary takes **antibiotics** for two weeks. The graph shows the number of **bacteria** in his blood during that time.

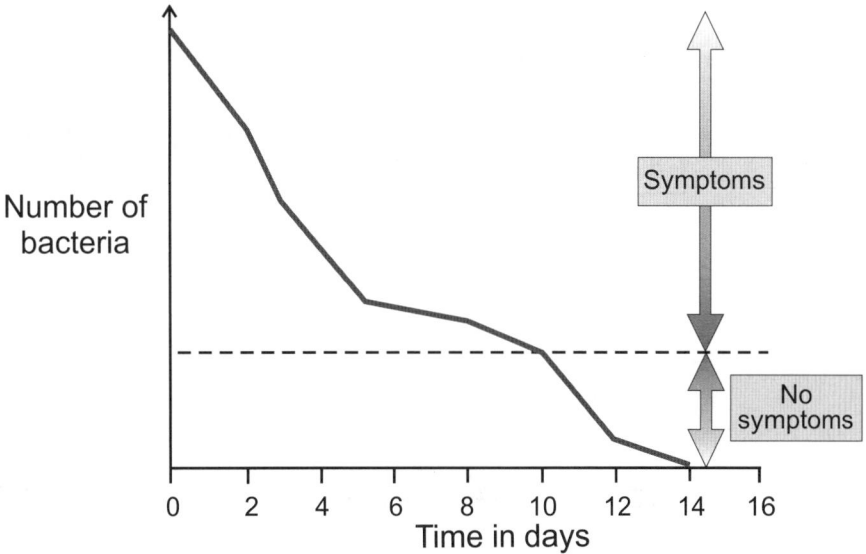

a) How many days did it take for Gary's symptoms to end? ....

b) Why is it important for Gary to finish his full course of antibiotics? Circle the answer.

> **So the antibiotics can kill any viruses as well as the bacteria.**   **Because the antibiotics have been paid for.**   **To make it harder for bacteria to become resistant to the antibiotics.**

Q5 Why **won't** your doctor give you **antibiotics** if you have a **virus**? Tick the answer.

> Antibiotics are too expensive to waste on viruses. ☐   Viruses don't make you ill. ☐
>
> Antibiotics don't kill viruses. ☐   Viruses feed on antibiotics. ☐

Module B2 — Keeping Healthy

Drug Trials

Q1 Write the numbers **1-3** in the boxes to show the **order** that a **drug** is **tested** in.

☐ Drug is tested on healthy human volunteers.

☐ Drug is tested on ill human volunteers.

☐ Drug is tested on human cells and animals in a laboratory.

Q2 a) Why are drugs **tested** on **healthy human volunteers**? Circle **one** answer.

| To look at what the drug is made from. | To check the drug is safe. | To see how much the drug costs. | To make sure the drug works. |

b) Why are drugs tested on **human cells** and **animals** in a laboratory? Circle **two** answers.

| To look at what the drug is made from. | To check the drug is safe. | To see how much the drug costs. | To make sure the drug works. |

Q3 **Placebos** are used in some drug trials.

a) What is a placebo? Circle the answer.

A drug that we know works.   A painkiller.   A type of energy drink.   A fake medicine that doesn't do anything.

b) Why are people given placebos in a drug trial? Tick the answer.

Placebos help check that it's really the drug making people better. ☐

Placebos help check that any side effects aren't because of the drug. ☐

c) Placebos aren't used in trials of drugs for treating people who are seriously ill. Tick the reason why.

☐ The results would be more useful if everyone took the drug.

☐ It wouldn't be fair to give a patient a placebo if there was a chance the drug could treat their illness.

☐ Placebos are expensive to make.

Module B2 — Keeping Healthy

The Circulatory System

Q1 The **heart** pumps blood around the body.

a) Which of the following is **true**? Circle the answer.

   The heart is a single pump.   The heart is a double pump.

b) Circle the right word in the sentences below.

   The **left / right** side of the heart pumps blood to the lungs.

   The **left / right** side of the heart pumps blood around the rest of the body.

c) What type of cells make up the heart? Circle the answer.

   stem cells   muscle cells   egg cells   memory cells

d) Name two things the blood brings to the heart cells.

   1. .... 2. ....

Q2 The pictures below show three **blood vessels**.

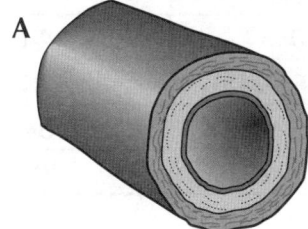  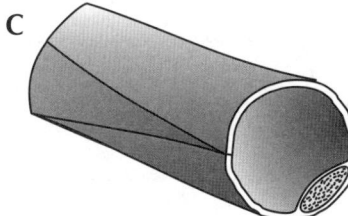

   A   B   C

a) Write the name of each blood vessel by the correct letter. Use the labels below.

   capillary   artery   vein

   A = ...   B = ...   C = ...

b) Draw lines to match the structures to their functions.

   STRUCTURE   FUNCTION

   thick, stretchy walls in arteries   to cope with high blood pressure

   thin walls in capillaries   to keep blood flowing in the right direction

   valves in veins   so things like food and oxygen can pass through easily

Module B2 — Keeping Healthy

Heart Rate and Blood Pressure

Q1 Circle the right words in the sentences below.

> Blood pressure measurements show how hard your blood is pushing against the wall of **a vein** / **an artery**. They're given as **two** / **four** numbers. The **higher** / **lower** number is the pressure when the heart contracts. The **higher** / **lower** number is the pressure when the heart relaxes.

Q2 Tick the box next to the statement which is **true**.

Your pulse rate is the number of pulses you feel in one hour. ☐

You can feel your pulse on the inside of your wrist. ☐

Your heart rate is three times higher than your pulse rate. ☐

Q3 The table shows the heart rates of five men. **Normal heart rates are in the range of 60 to 100 beats per minute.**

	Heart Rate (beats per minute)
Chris	70
Dan	44
Steve	76
Ahmed	64
Nigel	105

a) Which of the men has a high heart rate?

....

b) How many men have heart rates in the normal range?

....

c) Why are normal heart rates given as ranges? Circle the answer.

because individual people are different   because the scientists couldn't decide on a single figure   to show your heart rate when you're resting and exercising

Q4 **High blood pressure** can lead to a **heart attack**. Write numbers in the boxes to show how this happens. One has been done for you.

The artery becomes blocked. ☐

High blood pressure can damage an artery. ☐ 1

If the artery leads to the heart, it causes a heart attack. ☐

Lumps of fat (fatty deposits) can build up. ☐

Module B2 — Keeping Healthy

Heart Disease

Q1 Which of these people are **most** at **risk** of **heart disease**? Tick **four** answers.

☐ Anne — she's really stressed.
☐ James — he drinks too much alcohol.
☐ Carly — she gets regular exercise by playing netball.
☐ Michael — he has a poor diet.
☐ Hannah — she smokes.

Q2 Circle the right word in the sentence below.

> Regular exercise **increases** / **lowers** the risk of heart disease.

Q3 Heart disease is **less common** in **poorer countries** than in richer countries. Tick **two** explanations for this.

☐ People in poorer countries have a lower fat diet.
☐ Poorer people in poorer countries have to walk more.
☐ Poorer people in poorer countries eat lots of junk food.

Q4 Professor Cardio wants to find out about the **factors** that **increase** the **risk** of **heart disease**.

a) What could he do to find out about these factors? Tick the answer.

☐ He could give people a placebo.
☐ He could do a study.

b) Professor Cardio thinks people's **genes** can make them **more at risk** of heart disease. Is he right? Circle the answer.

yes   no

Module B2 — Keeping Healthy

Homeostasis and The Kidneys

Q1 **Homeostasis** is a process in the human body.

a) What does homeostasis do? Tick the answer.

☐ It controls the amount of blood in the body.

☐ It maintains control systems in the body.

☐ It keeps the conditions in the body steady.

b) Why is homeostasis important for **cells**?

| So that cells can break down antigens. | So that cells don't become clogged with cholesterol. | So that cells can work properly. |

c) Homeostasis uses information sent by **nerves**. What else carries information in homeostasis?

....

Q2 **Automatic control systems** keep conditions in the body steady. They're made up of three parts. Draw lines between each part and its job.

- Receptors — Get information from the processing centres. They then respond.
- Processing Centres — Notice changes in the body.
- Effectors — Get information about the changes. They then decide what to do.

Q3 Circle the right word in the sentence below.

The **kidneys / muscles** balance the level of waste in the body.

They also balance the level of **blood / water** in the body.

Billy the kid-ney

Q4 a) Why does the body need to **balance** how much **water** it has? Circle the answer.

So that genes can work properly.   So that cells can work properly.

b) How does water **come into** the body? Write down **two** ways.

....

Module B2 — Keeping Healthy

Controlling Water Content

Q1 The **concentration** of your urine depends on **how much water** is in your **blood**.

a) Draw lines to match the type of urine to its description.

Dilute urine — contains a little water

Concentrated urine — contains a lot of water

b) List two things that affect how much water there is in your blood.

1. ....

2. ....

c) Circle the right words in the sentences below.

> If you drink a lot you'll make **concentrated / dilute** urine.
>
> On a hot day you'll make **concentrated / dilute** urine.
>
> If you eat a lot of salt you'll make **concentrated / dilute** urine.

d) When you **exercise** you make more **concentrated urine**. Tick the reason why.

☐ You get hot and sweat. You lose water in your sweat. So you make more concentrated urine.

☐ Exercise stops you sweating. You stop losing water. So you make more concentrated urine.

Q2 Drinking **alcohol** can affect the amount of water in your urine.

a) Does drinking alcohol lead to **more concentrated** or **more dilute** urine?

....

b) Drinking alcohol can cause dehydration. What is **dehydration**? Circle the answer.

It's where you don't have enough water in your body.

It's where you have too much water in your body.

It's where your body makes its own water.

c) Give three things that dehydration can cause.

1. .... 2. .... 3. ....

d) What drug can affect the amount of water in the blood? Circle the answer.

painkillers   antibiotics   nicotine   ecstasy

Module B2 — Keeping Healthy

Mixed Questions — Module B2

Q1 Draw lines to match the **structures** with the type of **blood vessel** they're found in.

- valves
- thin walls
- thick, stretchy walls
- arteries
- capillaries
- veins

Q2 What factors can increase the risk of **heart disease**? Circle **three** answers.

smoking   exercise   poor diet   taking ecstasy

Q3 Do the following things make you produce **concentrated** or **dilute urine**?
Put ticks in the table to show your answers. The first one has been done for you.

	Concentrated urine	Dilute urine
Hot weather	✔	
Eating a lot of salt		
Drinking alcohol		
Taking ecstasy		

Q4 Helen has a **kidney infection**. It's caused by **bacteria**.

a) Could Helen be given antibiotics as a treatment? Tick the answer.

☐ Yes. Antibiotics can kill bacteria.

☐ No. Antibiotics can only kill viruses.

b) Why is it important that Helen takes the **full course** of antibiotics?

....

The bacteria that cause Helen's kidney infection can be grown in a lab.
A bacteria copies itself once every **20 minutes**. It's left for **60 minutes**.

c) How many times will the bacteria reproduce in 60 minutes? Circle the answer.

2   3   4   5

d) How many bacteria will there be at the end of 60 minutes? Circle the answer.

8   24   60

Use your answer to part a) to help you.

Module B2 — Keeping Healthy

Module B3 — Life on Earth

Adaptation and Variation

Q1 What is a **species**? Tick the answer.

- A group of organisms that are very different from each other. ☐
- A group of organisms that can breed together to make fertile offspring. ☐
- A group of organisms that live in the same place but can't breed together. ☐

Q2 Circle the right words in the sentences.

a) Adaptations are features that help organisms **mutate / survive** in their environment.

b) Members of a species are **more / less** likely to have offspring if the species is well adapted to its environment.

c) If a species has lots of offspring, the species is **more / less** likely to survive.

Q3 a) Individuals of a species are usually **different**. What is this called? Circle the answer.

evolution   adaptation   variation

b) Differences can be caused by **mutations**. What is a mutation? Tick the answer.

- A mutation is a change in heart rate. ☐
- A mutation is a change in the weather. ☐
- A mutation is a change in a gene. ☐

c) Circle the correct words to complete the sentences below.

Mutations in **muscle / sex** cells can be passed on to offspring.

This can cause offspring to develop **new features / acne**.

Natural Selection and Selective Breeding

Q1 Are these sentences **true** or **false**? Tick the boxes.

                                                                                                     True   False

    a) Living things vary.

    b) Species adapt to their environments by natural selection.

    c) Natural selection is carried out by humans.

    d) Individuals can pass on the genes that control their features to their offspring.

Q2 Circle the right words in the sentences below.

> Some individuals have features that make them more likely to **survive** / **decompose**.
>
> Individuals with these features are more likely to have **mutations** / **offspring**.
>
> This means they'll pass on the **blood cells** / **genes** that control these features.
>
> The useful features will become **more** / **less** common.

Q3 A farmer has found a way to grow bigger tomatoes.

    1. Choose the biggest tomatoes.
    2. Only breed the biggest tomatoes.
    3. All the baby tomatoes will be big.

    a) What is the name of this process? Circle the answer.

        natural breeding   genetics   natural selection   selective breeding

    b) This process different to natural selection. Tick **one** reason why.

> This process can only be used with plants.
>
> This process can be used to pass on features that don't help survival.
>
> This process always makes new species.

Module B3 — Life on Earth

Evolution

Q1 a) How long ago did **life on Earth** begin? Circle the answer.

350 thousand years

3500 million years

3500 billion years

b) Circle the word to complete this sentence.

All the species that have ever lived evolved from very **simple / complex** living things.

Q2 Tick the statement that is **true**.

New species are never made. ☐

Evolution can make new species. ☐

Extinction can make new species. ☐

Q3 Complete the sentences to show how **new species** are made. Use the words given below. The first one has been done for you.

Groups of organisms of the same species become ......*separated*...... .

separated   closer

a) If the environments .... the groups will develop different features.

change   stay the same

b) Some new features help the organisms ....

survive   mutate

c) .... makes these features more common.

selective breeding   natural selection

d) After a long time the groups become different ....

kingdoms   species

Module B3 — Life on Earth

Evolution

Q4 The **fossil record** is evidence of evolution.

a) What are fossils? Underline the answer.

Organisms that live in rock.   Organisms that live in volcanoes.

Dead organisms found in water.   Dead organisms found in rocks.

b) Does the fossil record show organisms getting more or less complex over time? Circle the answer.

more complex   less complex

c) Add the labels on the left to the diagram.

simple organisms   complex organisms

oldest

youngest

Age of fossil: ....

d) What else can scientists look at to study evolution? Circle the answer.

DNA   historical records   animal waste

Q5 a) Who came up with the **theory of evolution by natural selection**?

....

b) Lamarck had a different theory of evolution. He thought that features could be developed and then passed on to offspring. Why was Lamarck **wrong**? Tick the answer.

☐ Features can't ever be passed on to offspring.

☐ Developed features aren't useful enough to be passed on to offspring.

☐ Developed features aren't controlled by genes, so they can't be passed on to offspring.

Module B3 — Life on Earth

Biodiversity and Classification

Q1 a) What is **biodiversity**? Tick the answer.

- A way of making new species. ☐
- The variety of life on Earth. ☐
- A theory of evolution. ☐
- The number of extinct species. ☐

b) Which of these is **not** included in **biodiversity**? Circle the answer.

The history of a species.   The range of different types of organisms.

The genetic variation in a species.   The number of species.

c) Circle the word to complete this sentence.

Biodiversity **rises** / **falls** when a species becomes extinct.

Q2 Are these sentences **true** or **false**? Tick the boxes.

	True	False
a) A species is extinct when the number of individuals increases.	☐	☐
b) Some extinctions have been caused by humans.	☐	☐
c) The speed that species are becoming extinct is slowing down.	☐	☐
d) If we stop extinction, we're less likely to lose out on new crops and medicines.	☐	☐

Q3 All organisms can be **classified** into groups.

a) Draw lines to match the **group** with the **types of organism** and the **number of features in common**. One line has been drawn for you.

Group	Types of organism	Features in common
kingdom	one type of organism	few features in common
species	lots of types of organisms	lots of features in common

b) What can be used to group organisms together? Circle **two** answers.

physical features   size of population   DNA

Module B3 — Life on Earth

Energy in an Ecosystem

Q1 The diagram shows a **food chain**.

Tick **three** statements that are **true**.

A food chain is part of a food web.	☐
The arrows show what is eaten by what.	☐
The hedgehog is the first stage in this food chain.	☐
The snail in this food chain is eaten by the hedgehog.	☐

Q2 Circle the words to complete the sentences.

a) The energy in a food chain comes from the **Sun** / **Moon**.

b) Plants use the energy for **photosynthesis** / **respiration**.

c) Animals get energy by **decaying** / **eating** plants or other animals.

d) Decay organisms get energy when they feed on **living** / **dead** organisms.

leaf it out

Q3 **Energy** is **lost** at each stage of a food chain. Some energy is lost as **heat**.

a) Give two other ways energy can be lost from a food chain.

1. ....

2. ....

b) Why do you not normally get food chains with more than five stages? Circle the answer.

Because so much energy is lost at each stage.

Because not enough energy is made at each stage.

Because there aren't enough plants and animals to make a long chain.

Module B3 — Life on Earth

Energy in an Ecosystem

Q4 The diagram below shows the **energy** in a **food chain**.

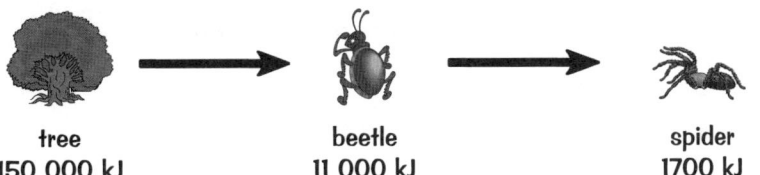

tree 150 000 kJ → beetle 11 000 kJ → spider 1700 kJ

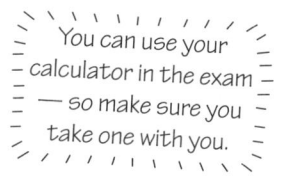
You can use your calculator in the exam — so make sure you take one with you.

a) How much energy is there in the **2nd stage** of the food chain? Tick the answer.

1700 kJ ☐   150 000 kJ ☐   11 000 kJ ☐

b) How much energy is there in the **3rd stage** of the food chain? Tick the answer.

1700 kJ ☐   150 000 kJ ☐   11 000 kJ ☐

c) How much energy is **lost** between the 2nd stage and the 3rd stage?

amount of energy lost = energy in the 2nd stage − energy in the 3rd stage

....

Q5 A **food chain** is shown in the diagram.

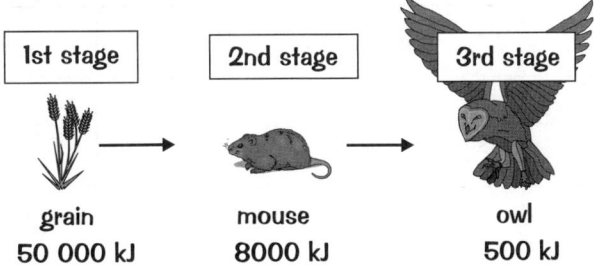

1st stage — grain 50 000 kJ → 2nd stage — mouse 8000 kJ → 3rd stage — owl 500 kJ

a) How much energy is there in the 1st stage of the food chain? Tick the answer.

500 kJ ☐   50 000 kJ ☐   8000 kJ ☐

b) How much energy is lost between the 1st stage and the 2nd stage?

amount of energy lost = energy in the 1st stage − energy in the 2nd stage

....

c) Calculate the **efficiency** of energy transfer from the 1st stage to the 2nd stage.

$$\text{efficiency} = \frac{\text{energy in the 2nd stage}}{\text{energy in the 1st stage}} \times 100$$

Your answer should be a percentage (%).

....

Module B3 — Life on Earth

Interactions Between Organisms

Q1 Circle the word to complete these sentences.

a) Organisms get all the resources they need from the **environment** / **Sun**.

b) Resources **are** / **aren't** limited.

Q2 Two species of spider (A and B) **only eat** the same type of fly.

a) What is it called when species fight with other species for resources?

    adaptation   competition   variation   extinction

b) Species B is better at catching the flies than species A. What might happen to species A? Circle your answer.

    It will get fat.   It will start cheating.   It won't survive.

Q3 The deer-cat only lives in one forest. The table shows how the number of deer-cats changed over **five years**.

Year	2006	2007	2008	2009	2010
Number of deer-cats	55	30	20	8	0

a) How many deer-cats were there in 2006? ....

b) How many deer-cats were there in 2009? ....

c) Which year was the deer-cat **extinct** in? Circle the answer.

    2006   2007   2008   2009   2010

d) What could have made the deer-cat extinct? Tick **four** answers.

- [ ] The environment might have changed.
- [ ] A new predator might have turned up.
- [ ] It might have been wiped out by a new disease.
- [ ] There may have been more food for the deer-cat.
- [ ] An organism it ate might have become extinct.

Module B3 — Life on Earth

Interactions Between Organisms

Q4 The diagram shows a **food web**.

a) What do the **voles** eat? Circle **two** answers.

   barn owls   ants   grass and seeds

b) What **eats the ants**? Circle **one** answer.

   barn owls   voles   grass and seeds

c) All the **voles die**. What will happen now?
   Circle the right words in the sentences below.

   The number of ants will **increase / decrease**.

   The number of barn owls will **increase / decrease**.

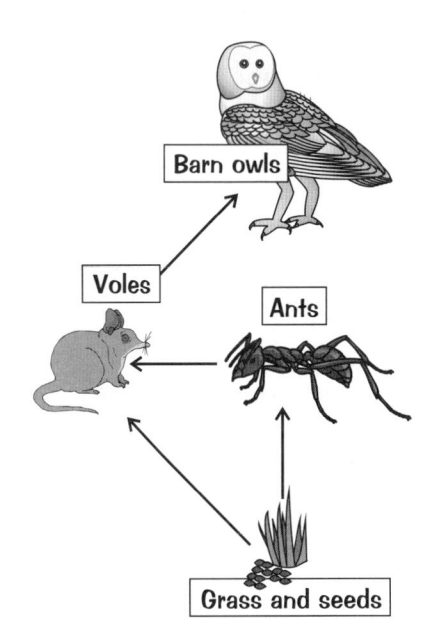

Q5 A **food web** is shown below.

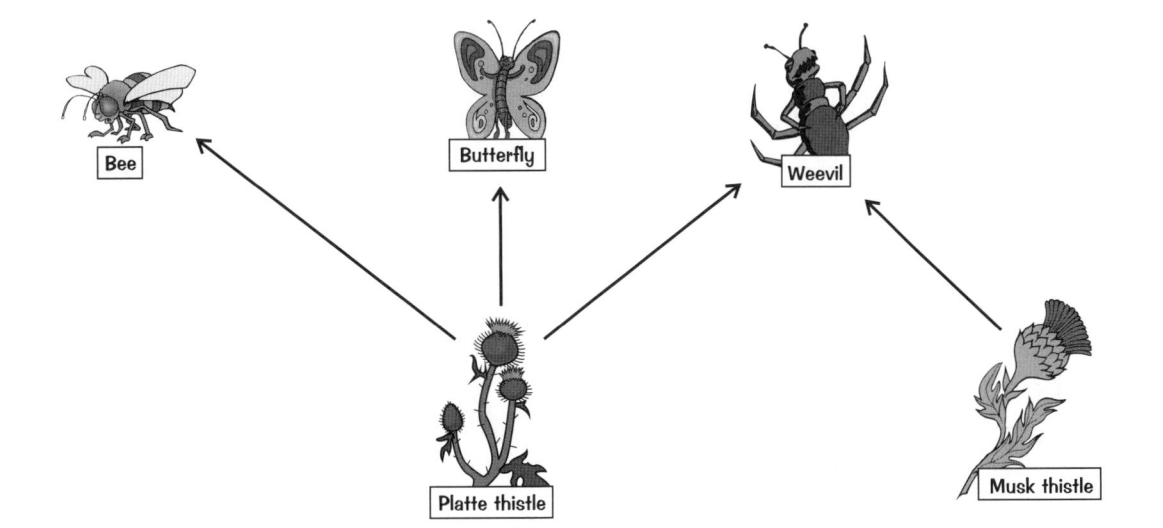

Fill in the blanks in the sentences using the words **more** or **fewer**.

If there are **more** platte thistles, there will be .... butterflies.

If there are **fewer** platte thistles, there will be .... bees.

If there are **more** weevils, there will be .... platte thistles.

Module B3 — Life on Earth

The Carbon Cycle

Q1 Plants use **carbon dioxide** in the air to make **sugars**.

a) Circle the correct word to complete the sentence below.

> Plants turn carbon into sugars by **respiration** / **photosynthesis**.

b) How are sugars passed from plants to animals? Circle the answer.

    by breathing   by photosynthesis   by decomposition   by feeding

c) Microorganisms **break down** dead plants and animals. What are these microorganisms called?

....

d) Tick the sentence that is **true**.

- Decomposition releases microorganisms into the air. ☐
- Decomposition releases carbon dioxide into the air. ☐
- Decomposition takes in carbon dioxide from the air. ☐

Q2 Add the labels to the diagram below. Write the letters in the boxes.

> **A** — Burning   **B** — Respiration   **C** — Photosynthesis

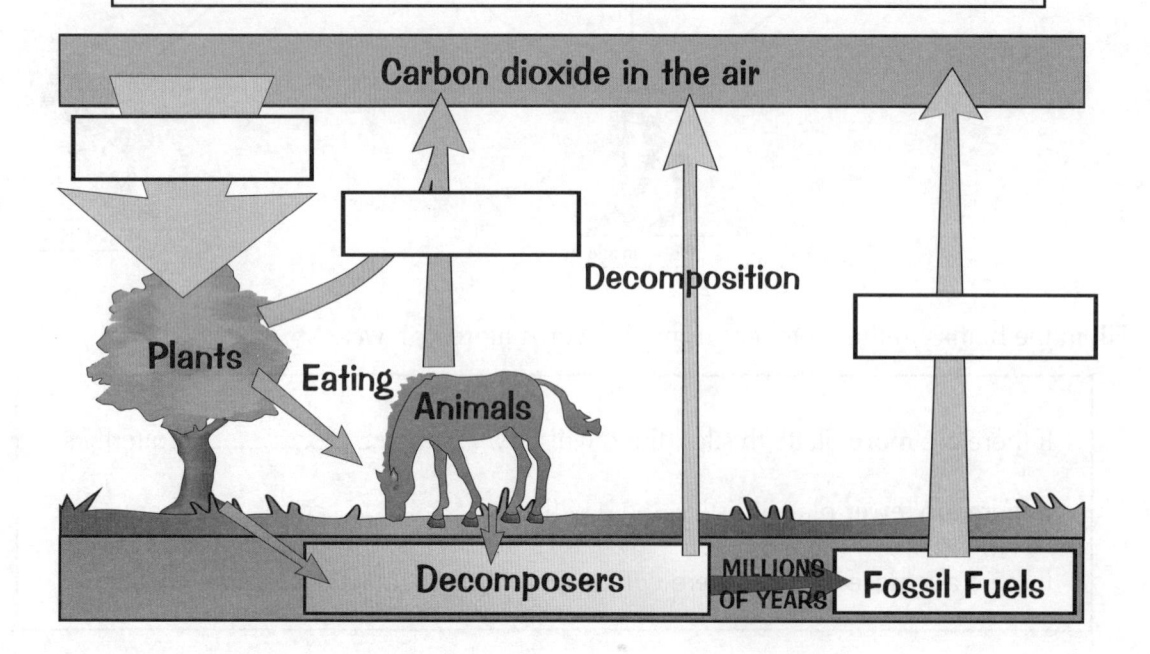

Module B3 — Life on Earth

The Nitrogen Cycle

Q1 Draw lines to match the type of **organism** with how they get **nitrogen**.

TYPE OF ORGANISM | HOW THEY GET NITROGEN

Plants — By eating

Animals — From nitrates in the soil

Q2 The diagram below shows the **nitrogen cycle**.

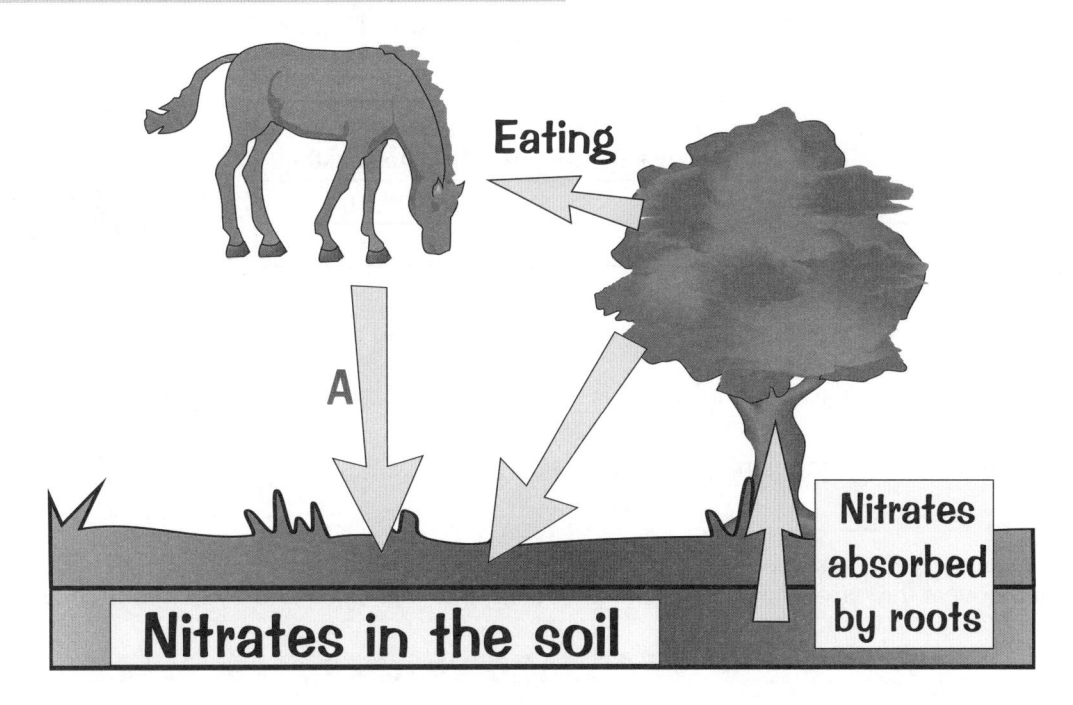

a) What is process **A** on the diagram? Underline the answer.

   decomposition   photosynthesis   eating   respiration

b) What do **decomposers** do in the nitrogen cycle?

....

c) Which sentence is **true**? Tick the answer.

- Animals break down dead plants to get nitrogen. ☐
- Breaking down dead plants and animals adds nitrogen to the soil. ☐
- Breaking down dead plants and animals takes nitrogen out of the air. ☐

Module B3 — Life on Earth

Measuring Environmental Change

Q1 Are these sentences **true** or **false**? Tick the boxes.

	True	False
a) Environmental change can be measured with non-living indicators.	☐	☐
b) Changes in nitrate level can show changes in water pollution.	☐	☐
c) Changes in carbon dioxide level don't show changes in air pollution.	☐	☐
d) Changes in temperature can be measured using thermometers.	☐	☐

Q2 a) Circle the correct word in the sentence below.

Mayfly nymphs and phytoplankton are **living indicators / decomposers**.

b) The table shows the numbers of mayfly nymphs and phytoplankton in polluted and unpolluted water.

Water type	Number of mayfly nymphs	Number of phytoplankton
Polluted	3	20
Unpolluted	23	7

Fill in the blanks in the sentences below using the words in the box.

Water with a lot of mayfly nymphs in it is ....

Water with a lot of phytoplankton in it is ....

polluted
unpolluted

Q3 **Lichen** covers three trees. The percentage of each tree that's covered by lichen is shown below.

Power Plant

Tree 1 — 18% of tree covered by lichen.

Tree 2 — 26% of tree covered by lichen.

Tree 3 — 38% of tree covered by lichen.

a) Which tree is covered most by lichen?

....

b) Why does the percentage of lichen cover **increase** further away from the power plant?

There are fewer predators.

There is more sewage.   The air is cleaner.

Power plants cause air pollution.

Module B3 — Life on Earth

Sustainability

Q1 What is **sustainability**? Tick the answer.

Harming the environment so people in the future **can't** get what they need. ☐

Letting people get what they need now **without harming** the environment. This is so people in the future **can** get what they need. ☐

Letting people get what they need now **without thinking** about how people in the future will cope. ☐

Q2 Circle the right words in the sentences below.

Some resources **aren't sustainable**. For example, **fossil fuels / wind power**.

They **will / won't** run out. This means people in the future **will / won't** be able to use them.

Other resources **are sustainable**. For example, **fossil fuels / wind power**.

They **will / won't** run out. This means people in the future **will / won't** be able to use them.

Q3 A farmer **only grows potatoes** in his fields.

    a) What this type of crop production called? Circle the answer.

        selective breeding   monoculture   evolution

    b) Is this type of crop production sustainable? Write '**yes**' or '**no**'.

    ....

    c) Nick and Sophie are talking about how this type of crop production affects **biodiversity**. Only one of them is right.

Nick: It's bad for biodiversity. Not many different species can survive if there's only one crop in the fields.

Sophie: It's good for biodiversity. It means lots of one crop can be grown.

Who is right, Nick or Sophie? ....

Module B3 — Life on Earth

Sustainability

Q4 a) Why is most packaging **not sustainable**? Circle the answer.

It's made from biodegradable materials.   We throw it away.

We reuse it.   It doesn't need energy to make it.

b) How can we make packaging more sustainable? Tick **two** boxes.

- [ ] Use renewable materials to make the packaging.
- [ ] Make all our packaging from plastic.
- [ ] Create lots of pollution while making the packaging.
- [ ] Use less energy to make the packaging.

Q5 **Plastic** and **cardboard** are packaging materials.

	Plastic	Cardboard
What is it made from?	Oil	Trees
Will this resource run out?	Yes	No
Does it break down naturally?	No	Yes

a) Why will cardboard not run out? Circle the answer.

More trees can be planted.   Cardboard never breaks.

b) Tick the box next to the sentence that is **true**.

Cardboard is biodegradable. [ ]

All plastic is biodegradable. [ ]

c) Look at the table. Which material is more sustainable?

....

d) Why are neither cardboard or plastic totally sustainable? Circle the answer.

They're too weak to use for packaging.   Making and transporting them uses energy.   They can't be recycled.   We don't use enough of them.

Module B3 — Life on Earth

Mixed Questions — Module B3

Q1 Draw lines to match the **process** to its **effect**.

PROCESS   EFFECT

Respiration — Takes carbon dioxide out of the air.

Photosynthesis — Releases carbon dioxide into the air.

Q2 Jack grows **grapes** on his farm.

a) Jack wants to make his grapes **bigger** and **juicier**. How could he do this? Circle the answer.

natural selection   competition   adaptation   selective breeding

b) Jack packages his grapes and sells them. How he could make his packaging **sustainable**? Circle the answer.

use lots of packaging   use packaging made from recycled materials

c) The grapes that Jack doesn't sell **decompose**. Name two things released by decomposition.

1. ....

2. ....

Q3 A **food chain** is shown.

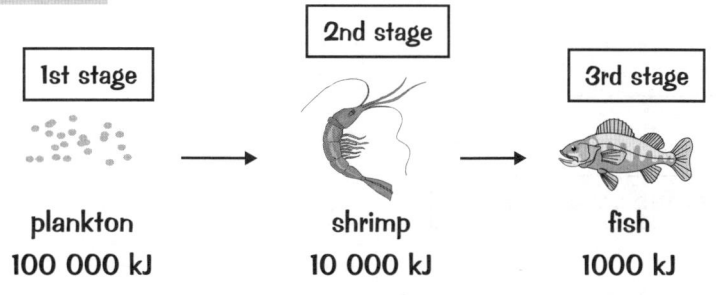

1st stage — plankton — 100 000 kJ

2nd stage — shrimp — 10 000 kJ

3rd stage — fish — 1000 kJ

Work out the **efficiency** of energy transfer from the 1st stage to the 2nd stage.

$$\text{efficiency} = \frac{\text{energy in the 2nd stage}}{\text{energy in the 1st stage}} \times 100$$

....

Module B3 — Life on Earth

Module C1 — Air Quality

How the Air was Made

Q1 Which of the sentences below is **true**? Tick **one** box.

The air was made when volcanoes gave out gases. ☐

The Earth's early atmosphere was mostly oxygen. ☐

Volcanoes only gave out water vapour. ☐

The air under the ground is called the atmosphere. ☐

Q2 Circle the right words in the sentences below.

a) Plants **took in** / **gave out** oxygen during photosynthesis.

b) Plants **took in** / **gave out** carbon dioxide during photosynthesis.

c) Lots of carbon dioxide **evaporated** / **dissolved** into the oceans.

d) Some **carbon dioxide** / **water vapour** was buried in sedimentary rocks.

e) The amount of carbon dioxide in the air has gone **up** / **down**.

f) The amount of oxygen in the air has gone **up** / **down**.

Q3 Write numbers in the boxes to put the sentences in the **right order**. The first one has been done for you.

☐ The Earth cooled down.

☐ Water vapour turned into liquid water.

[1] The Earth was really hot.

☐ Volcanoes gave out carbon dioxide and water vapour.

☐ The liquid water made the oceans.

The Air Today

Q1 a) Draw lines to match up the gases to how much there is in the air.

nitrogen — 1%

oxygen — 21%

argon — 78%

b) Name **two** other gases that are in the air.

1. ....

2. ....

Q2 Write out the sentences in the table to show if **pollutants** are added to the air by **humans** or **natural processes**.

Cars give out pollutants

Power stations give out pollutants

Volcanoes give out pollutants

Human activity	Natural process

Q3 Circle the substances below that are **pollutants**. Circle **five** answers.

nitrogen   sulfur dioxide   argon   oxygen

carbon dioxide   nitrogen oxides   particulates   carbon monoxide

Q4 Pollutants can cause acid rain and carbon monoxide poisoning. Draw lines to show whether these harm **people**, harm the **environment**, or harm **both**.

acid rain

harms people

carbon monoxide poisoning

harms the environment

Module C1 — Air Quality

Chemical Reactions

Q1 Are there the correct number of **atoms** on each side of these reactions? Tick the right boxes.

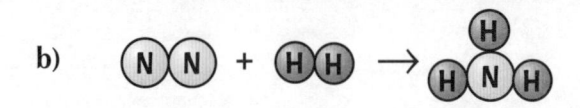

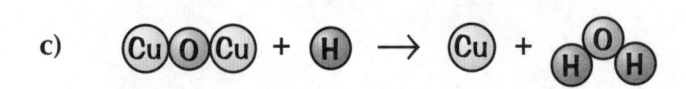

correct   incorrect

a) C C + O O → C O C O

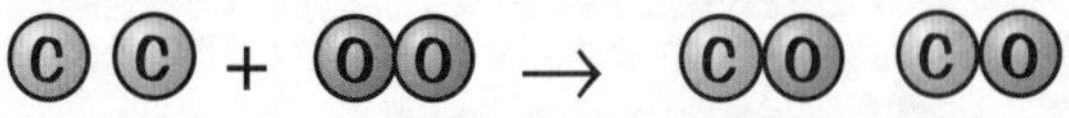

b) N N + H H → H N H with H on top (NH₃)

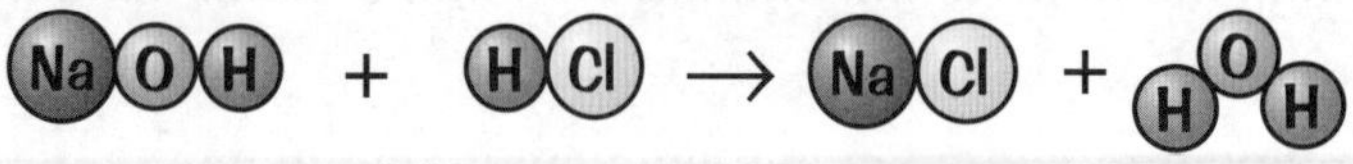

c) Cu O Cu + H → Cu + H O H

d) Na O H + H Cl → Na Cl + H O H

e) H C H (with H H) + O O O O → O C O + H O H H O H

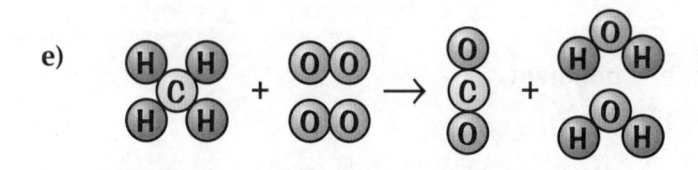

Q2 Use the words to fill in the gaps in the sentences. You will need to use one of the words **twice**.

molecules   mixture   spaces   atoms

Everything is made from tiny particles called ....

.... are atoms joined together.

Air is a .... of different gases.

Air is made of small ....

The molecules have large .... between them.

Q3 Which bubble (A or B) shows how the **molecules** in **air** can be drawn? Circle the right letter.

A   B

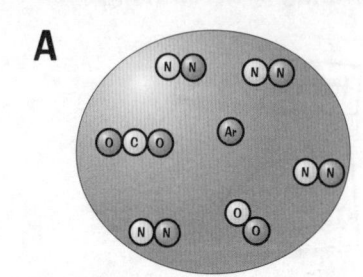

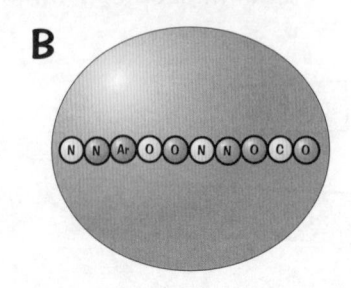

Module C1 — Air Quality

Chemical Reactions

Q4 a) Add the labels '**reactants**' and '**products**' to the reaction below.

Na Na + Cl Cl → Na Cl Na Cl

....

b) Which of the sentences below is **true**? Put a tick in the box.

☐ The properties of the products are the same as the properties of the reactants.

☐ The properties of the products are different from the properties of the reactants.

Properties are things like whether it's a gas, liquid or solid, or whether it conducts heat.

Q5 Are these sentences **true** or **false**? Tick the right boxes.

	True	False
Atoms can get lost in reactions.	☐	☐
There are always the same number of atoms at the start and the end of a reaction.	☐	☐
Atoms get swapped around in chemical reactions.	☐	☐
The number of atoms gets smaller in a chemical reaction.	☐	☐

Q6 a) Name the **reactants** and **products** in the reaction below.

hydrogen   oxygen   water

Reactants: ....   Product: ....

b) Fill in the table to show how many atoms there are in the reactants and products above. One has been done for you.

	reactants	products
number of hydrogen atoms	4	
number of oxygen atoms		

Module C1 — Air Quality

Fuels

Q1 Circle **three** fuels below that are made of hydrocarbons.

petrol   coal   diesel   fuel oil

Q2 Are these sentences **true** or **false**? Tick the right boxes.

		True	False
a)	When coal burns you get oxygen.	☐	☐
b)	Hydrocarbons are made of carbon and hydrogen atoms.	☐	☐
c)	Burning is also called combustion.	☐	☐
d)	Coal is a hydrocarbon.	☐	☐
e)	When a fuel burns, sometimes you get carbon dioxide and water.	☐	☐

Q3 Circle the right word in the sentences below.

> An oxidation reaction is a reaction where oxygen is **added / lost**.
>
> A reduction reaction is a reaction where oxygen is **added / lost**.

Q4 Which reaction shows a fuel **burning**? Tick the right box.

☐ 1.

☐ 2.

When a fuel burns, its atoms join with oxygen.

Q5 Fuels can be burnt in **pure oxygen** or **air**.

a) Do fuels burn faster in pure oxygen or air?

....

b) Would an oxy-fuel welding torch use pure oxygen or air?

....

Module C1 — Air Quality

Air Pollution — Carbon

Q1 Circle the right words in the sentences below.

a) Cars and power stations burn **carbon dioxide / fossil fuels**.

b) **Carbon dioxide / oxygen** is made when fuels burn.

c) Carbon particles fall down as **soot / carbon monoxide**.

d) When there's not much oxygen, you get **complete / incomplete** burning.

e) Carbon monoxide is made by **complete / incomplete** burning.

Q2 Use the formulas and diagrams in the box to fill in the table. Two have been done for you.

Name	Diagram	Formula
carbon monoxide	C O	
water		H_2O
carbon dioxide		

Q3 **Carbon dioxide** can be removed from the air.

a) How do **plants** remove carbon dioxide from the air? Circle the answer.

Combustion   Pollution   Photosynthesis

b) Give **one other** way that carbon dioxide is removed from the air.

....

Module C1 — Air Quality

Air Pollution — Sulfur and Nitrogen

Q1 Use the words below to fill in the gaps in the sentences. You can use the words more than once.

air   sulfur   sulfur dioxide

Fossil fuels sometimes have .... in them.

When the fuel burns, the .... burns too.

The pollutant .... is made.

It goes into the ....

Q2 Draw lines to join up the diagrams with the name of the pollutant.

Nitrogen monoxide

Nitrogen dioxide

Sulfur dioxide

Q3 Write out the **formulas** for the molecules below. One has been done for you.

nitrogen monoxide   **NO**

a) nitrogen dioxide   ....

b) sulfur dioxide   ....

Q4 Use the words below to fill in the labels on the diagram.

nitrogen oxides   nitrogen   oxygen

a) ....

+

b) ....   c) ....

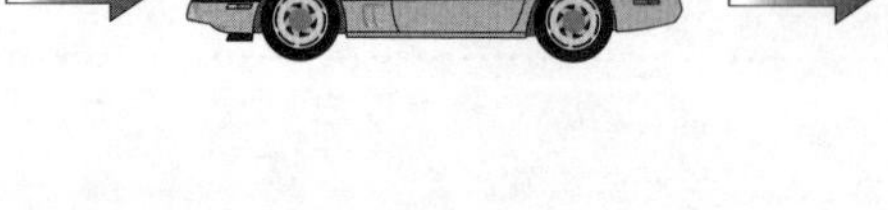

Module C1 — Air Quality

Air Pollution — Sulfur and Nitrogen

Q5 Tick the sentence that is **true** in each of the pairs below.

a) ☐ Nitrogen pollution comes from fuel.
   ☐ Nitrogen pollution comes from nitrogen in the air.

b) ☐ The temperature inside car engines is so high that nitrogen and oxygen react.
   ☐ The temperature inside car engines is so low that nitrogen and oxygen react.

c) ☐ Nitrogen oxides are pollutants.
   ☐ Nitrogen oxides aren't pollutants.

Q6 Are these sentences **true** or **false**? Tick the right boxes.

		True	False
a)	Oxides of nitrogen can cause acid rain.	☐	☐
b)	Sulfur dioxide can cause acid rain.	☐	☐
c)	Acid rain can kill plants and animals.	☐	☐

Q7 Number the boxes **1**, **2** and **3** to show the correct order.

☐ Acid rain falls. It kills plants and animals.

☐ Factories make sulfur dioxide pollution.

☐ The gas reacts with water in a clean cloud. Acid rain is made.

Module C1 — Air Quality

Reducing Pollution

Q1 Circle the right words in the sentences below.

> Using less electricity means **less** / **more** fossil fuels are burned.
>
> This means **less** / **more** carbon dioxide is given out.

Q2 a) Which gases do catalytic converters **remove** from the exhaust gases of cars? Circle **two** gases.

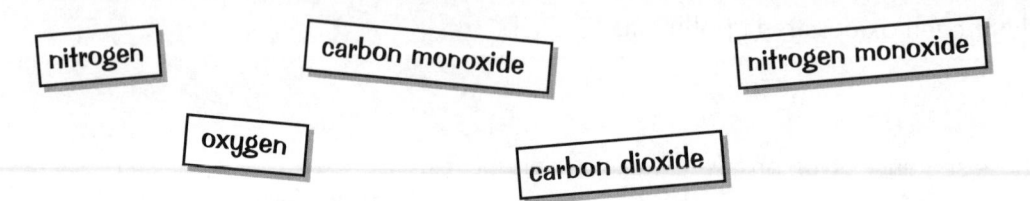

nitrogen   carbon monoxide   nitrogen monoxide   oxygen   carbon dioxide

b) Which gases do catalytic converters give out? Circle **two** gases.

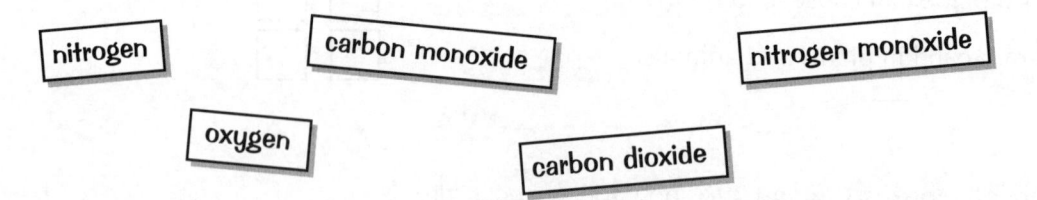

nitrogen   carbon monoxide   nitrogen monoxide   oxygen   carbon dioxide

Q3 a) Is it better for the environment if people use **cars** or **public transport**?

....

b) Why would this make less pollution?

....

Q4 Complete the sentences below using the words given underneath them.

a) Efficient engines burn .... fuel than old engines.

less   more   the same amount of

b) This means that they make .... pollution.

more   less   the same amount of

Module C1 — Air Quality

Reducing Pollution

Q5 George's car had an **exhaust emission** check as part of its **MOT test**. George's car had the following test results:

Don't worry about the units.

	George's car	Level of emissions allowed
Carbon monoxide level	0.2%	0.3%
Hydrocarbon level	4 ppm	200 ppm

a) Circle the right words in the sentence below.

Cars that make **too much** / **too little** pollution will fail their MOT test.

b) Did George's car give out more or less **carbon monoxide** than the level allowed?

....

c) Did George's car give out more or less **hydrocarbons** than the level allowed?

....

d) Did George's car pass the exhaust emissions part of the MOT test?

....

Q6 Use the words below to complete the sentences. You will need to use **one word** more than once.

> sulfur dioxide   fuel oil
> clean   pollutant   particulate carbon

a) Sulfur dioxide is a ....

b) To reduce sulfur dioxide pollution you could take the sulfur out of the ....

that power stations use. This means that less .... is given out.

c) You can .... the gas coming out of coal-burning power stations.

This means that less .... and less .... is given out.

Module C1 — Air Quality

Mixed Questions — Module C1

Q1 Which of the sentences below describes what happens when a **hydrocarbon** is **burned**? Circle A, B, C or D.

    A   Oxygen is made.

    B   Carbon dioxide and oxygen are made.

    C   Carbon dioxide and water are made.

    D   Water and oxygen are made.

Q2 What is an **oxidation reaction**? Circle the correct answer.

    Any reaction where oxygen is added.

    Any reaction where oxygen is removed.   Any reaction where there is oxygen.

Q3 a) Name the **two** substances that are only made in **incomplete burning**.

    1. ....

    2. ....

b) Tick the boxes next to the diagrams that show these two substances.

Q4 Complete the sentences below by circling the right words.

    Cars have been made to produce less **pollution / power**.

    New vehicles can use low **sulfur / oxygen** fuels.

    When engines are more efficient they burn **less / more** fuel.

    Engines can have **catalytic converters / noise reducers** put in them.

    These change some of the **fuels / gases** that cars give out.

Module C1 — Air Quality

Mixed Questions — Module C1

Q5 The graphs below give information about the Earth's atmosphere millions of years ago and today.

Use the graphs to answer the following questions.

a) How has the level of carbon dioxide changed? Circle the answer.

it has gone up   it has gone down   it has stayed the same

b) How has the level of nitrogen changed? Circle the answer.

it has gone up   it has gone down   it has stayed the same

c) How has the level of oxygen changed? Circle the answer.

it has gone up   it has gone down   it has stayed the same

Q6 What is a **chemical reaction**? Tick the correct box.

☐ A chemical reaction is when atoms are made.

☐ A chemical reaction is when atoms are rearranged.

☐ A chemical reaction is when atoms are lost.

Q7 Are these sentences **true** or **false**? Tick the right boxes.

	True	False
a) The atmosphere is now mostly made up from nitrogen.	☐	☐
b) Volcanoes only gave out oxygen and water vapour.	☐	☐
c) Human activity gives out carbon dioxide and sulfur dioxide.	☐	☐
d) Acid rain is made from carbon monoxide.	☐	☐

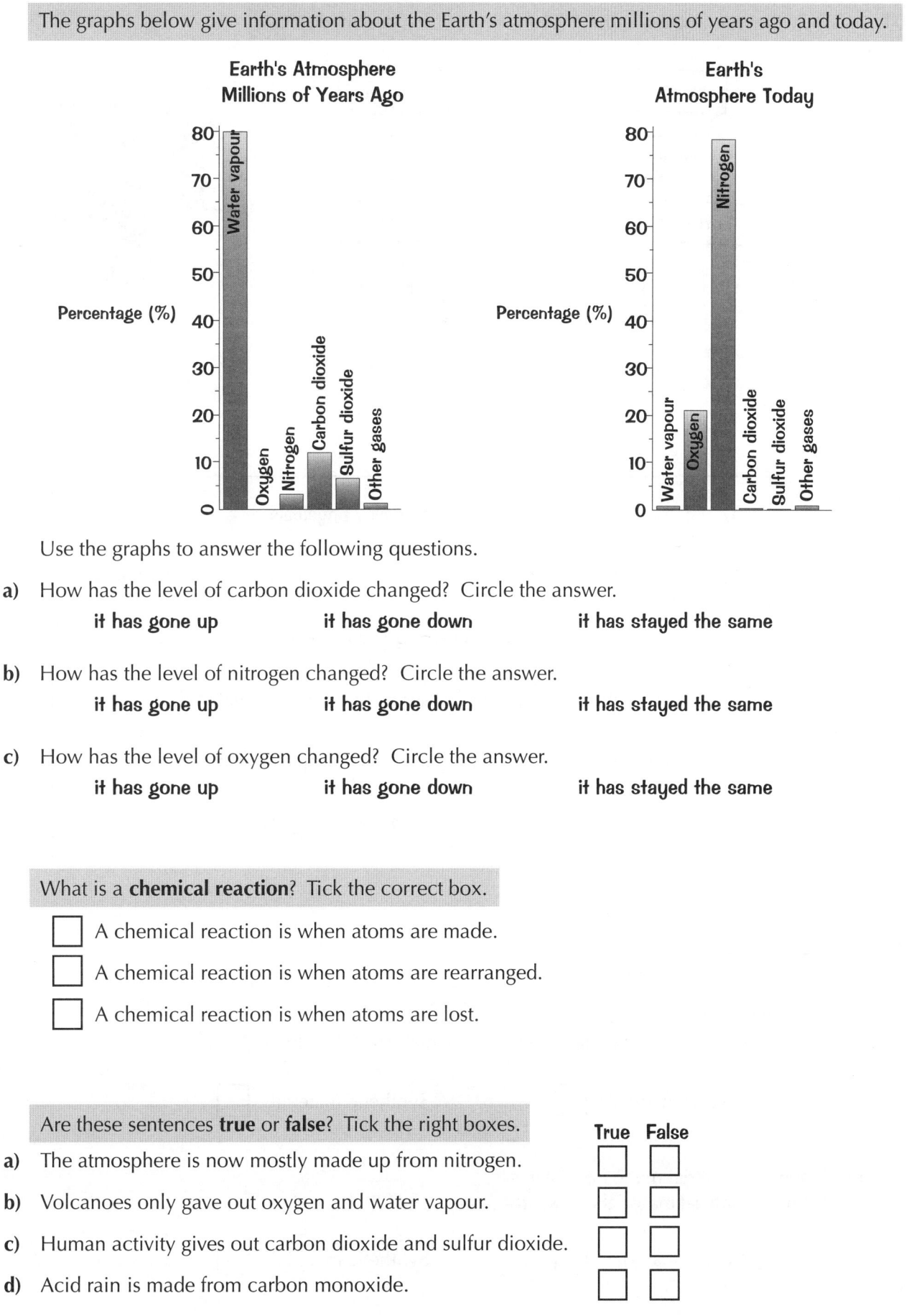

Module C1 — Air Quality

Natural and Synthetic Materials

Q1 Draw lines to match the **materials** with what they are **made from**.

- paper
- wool
- cotton
- silk

- silk worms
- trees
- sheep
- plants

Q2 Complete the sentences by circling the right word in each pair.

a) All materials are made up of **chemicals** / **physicals**.

b) A material with more than one chemical in it is called a **group** / **mixture**.

c) Metals, polymers and **ceramics** / **pyramids** are all types of material.

d) Materials made by humans are **synthetic** / **symbolic** materials.

e) Materials from the Earth's crust are called **simple** / **raw** materials.

f) Natural materials are made by **living** / **non-living** things.

Q3 Materials can be **natural** or **synthetic**.

a) **Polyester** is a material made by scientists in a lab.
Is polyester a **natural material** or a **synthetic material**? Tick the right box.

Natural material ☐   Synthetic material ☐

b) **Linen** is a material made from plants.
Is linen a **natural material** or a **synthetic material**? Tick the right box.

Natural material ☐   Synthetic material ☐

Module C2 — Material Choices

Materials and Properties

Q1 Complete the sentences by circling the right word in each pair.

a) You can find out how strong something is by seeing how easy it is to **break** / **move** it.

b) You can also test how strong something is by seeing how easy it is to change its **size** / **shape**.

c) A material that has good tension strength can stand up to **pulling** / **pushing** forces.

d) A stiff material will be **easy** / **hard** to bend.

Q2 Look at the diagram below. Then complete the sentences by circling the right word in each pair.

Melting point of sodium chloride 801 °C
Melting point of sulfur 115 °C
20 °C
Melting point of water 0 °C

a) At 20 °C sodium chloride is a **solid** / **liquid**.

b) At 20 °C sulfur is a **solid** / **liquid**.

c) At 20 °C water is a **solid** / **liquid**.

Q3 Tick the boxes to show whether the sentences are **true** or **false**.

	True	False
a) Density is how much stuff there is in a certain amount of space.	☐	☐
b) In a dense material the particles are spread out.	☐	☐
c) If the particles of a material are close together it is not very dense.	☐	☐

Q4 Diamond has a high **compressive strength**.

a) Circle the right word in the sentence below.

Compressive strength is how well a material can stand up to **pulling** / **pushing** forces.

b) Why are **diamonds** used to make the end of **drills**? Circle the answer below.

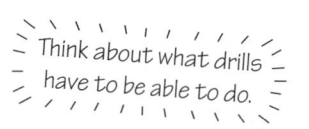

Think about what drills have to be able to do.

A Diamond doesn't conduct electricity

B Diamond is very hard

C Diamond is very soft

D Diamond is very dense

Module C2 — Material Choices

Materials, Properties and Uses

Q1 Draw a line to match each item with the best material to make it from. Use each material once.

diving suit   child's toy plane   window pane   washing line

Material A	Material B	Material C	Material D
strong	made from fibres	waterproof	hard
brightly coloured	bendy	soft	strong
easy to mould	high tension strength	bendy	see-through

Q2 Draw lines to match each sentence with the right ending.

Fibres are used to make clothes because they are...   ...strong and bendy.

Plastic is used to make TV cases because it is...   ...soft and strong.

Rubber is used for making car tyres because it is...   ...stiff and hard.

Q3 Choose the **right material** for each use.

materials: Plastic   China   Ice   Metal

a) Teapots need to keep heat in and not melt when they get hot. What should they be made from? ....

b) Statues need to last a long time. What should they be made from? ....

c) Shopping bags need to be strong and light. What should they be made from? ....

Q4 A new material has been made. It is **strong** and **soft**, but **not waterproof**.

a) What would it be **most useful** for making? Circle your answer.

     rain coat   pyjamas   shirt buttons

b) Give **one** reason why the material is not good for making **tents**.

Think about where a tent is used.

....

....

Module C2 — Material Choices

Crude Oil

Q1 Tick the box to show what **hydrocarbons** are made of.

carbon and hydrogen ☐   carbon and chlorine ☐   carbon and oxygen ☐

Q2 Complete the sentences by circling the right word in each pair.

a) The hydrocarbon chains in crude oil are held together by **forces / molecules**.

b) Long hydrocarbons have **more / fewer** forces holding the chains together than short hydrocarbons.

c) It takes lots of energy to break **short / long** hydrocarbon chains apart.

d) Long hydrocarbons have **higher / lower** boiling points than short hydrocarbons.

Q3 Propane and decane are both hydrocarbons.
Propane has **3** carbon atoms. **Decane** has **10** carbon atoms.

a) Draw a line to join each name to the right diagram.

propane   decane

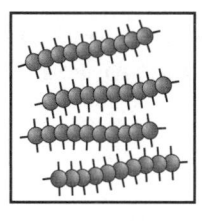

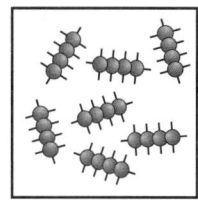

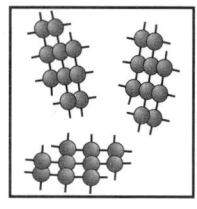

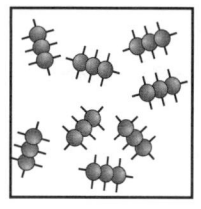

b) Which hydrocarbon will have **more forces** between its molecules? Circle the answer.

propane   decane

Remember — propane has 3 carbon atoms, decane has 10.

c) Which hydrocarbon will need **less energy** to turn from liquid into gas? Circle the answer.

propane   decane

d) Which hydrocarbon will have a **higher boiling point**? Circle the answer.

propane   decane

Module C2 — Material Choices

Uses of Crude Oil

Q1 Draw lines to join the **uses** of crude oil with the **descriptions**.

Fuels — Can help make machinery run smoothly.

Raw materials — Can be burnt to release energy.

Lubricants — Are used to make new chemicals.

Q2 Complete the passage by choosing words from the list below.

> hydrocarbons   fraction   refining   boiling point
>
> Crude oil can be split up into groups. This is called ....
>
> The oil is split up into groups of ....
>
> The molecules in each group have about the same ....
>
> Each group is called a ....

Q3 Each of the sentences below has **one mistake** in it. The mistakes are shown in **bold**. Write out each sentence so it is correct. The first one has been done for you.

a) Crude oil straight from the ground is **more** useful than refined oil.

   Crude oil straight from the ground is less useful than refined oil.

b) Separating **petrol** into fractions is called refining.

   ....

c) Refining is done using **divisional** distillation.

   ....

d) Fractions are groups of hydrocarbons with **different** boiling points.

   ....

e) Most crude oil is made into **lubricants**.

   ....

Module C2 — Material Choices

Polymerisation

Q1 Circle the letter next to what **polymerisation** means.

- A Lots of small molecules joining to form long molecules.
- B Lots of small atoms joining to form large atoms.
- C Long molecules breaking up into lots of small molecules.
- D Large atoms breaking up into lots of small atoms.

Q2 Fill in the gaps in the passage below using the following words.

| monomers | polymerisation | molecules |

Plastics are made up of polymers. These are giant ....

They are made by joining small molecules called .... together.

The reaction that is used to make polymers is called ....

Q3 Tick the boxes to show whether the statements are **true** or **false**.

	True	False
a) You can make lots of different polymers.	☐	☐
b) All polymers have very similar properties.	☐	☐

We bring you gold, frankincense... and poly-myrrh.

Q4 Some polymers have **better properties** than older materials. So the polymer might be used **instead** of the older material.

a) Give one example of an **older material** and name a **new material** that is now used instead.

Older material: ....

New material: ....

b) Give **one** advantage of using this new material instead of the older material.

....

....

Module C2 — Material Choices

Structure and Properties of Polymers

Q1 Tick the boxes to show whether the statements are **true** or **false**.

True False

a) What a polymer is like depends on the way it's made. ☐ ☐

b) Polymer chains are held together by forces. ☐ ☐

c) All polymers are held together by weak forces. ☐ ☐

d) If you change the length of a polymer its properties will change. ☐ ☐

Properties are things like whether it's stiff or bendy.

Q2 Complete the following sentences by circling the right word from each pair.

a) Polymer chains are held **together** / **apart** by forces between the chains.

b) If these forces are weak, a **lot** / **bit** of energy is needed to separate the chains. This makes the polymer **easy** / **hard** to stretch.

c) If these forces are strong, a **lot** / **bit** of energy is needed to separate the chains. This makes the polymer **easy** / **hard** to stretch.

d) The stronger the forces between the polymer chains, the **lower** / **higher** the melting point.

Q3 The diagrams below show how polymer X has been **changed** to make polymer Y.

polymer X   polymer Y

a) How is polymer X **different** to polymer Y?

....

b) Which polymer will be **stiffer**?

....

c) Which polymer will have the **higher melting point**?

....

Module C2 — Material Choices

Structure and Properties of Polymers

Q4 Polymers can be **changed** to give them **different properties**. Circle **two** ways that this can be done.

shake them about   add cross-linking

decrease the chain length   heat them up

Q5 The diagrams below show the structures of two **different polymers**.

Polymer A   Polymer B

a) Which polymer has **cross-links**? Tick the right box.

☐ polymer A   ☐ polymer B

b) What do **cross-links do**? Tick the right box.

☐ push polymer chains apart   ☐ hold polymer chains together

c) Which polymer will be **stiffer** and **stronger**? Tick the right box.

☐ polymer A   ☐ polymer B

Q6 Polythene can be made from **short-chain** or **long-chain** polymers.

Complete the list below to show the **properties** of **long-chain polythene**. The first one has been done for you.

SHORT-CHAIN POLYTHENE	LONG-CHAIN POLYTHENE
easy to stretch	1. harder to stretch
floppy	2. ....
low melting point	3. ....

Module C2 — Material Choices

Nanotechnology

Q1 **Nanoparticles** are **very small** particles.

a) How big are nanoparticles? Circle the correct answer.

less than 1 nanometre   1 – 100 nanometres   100 – 1000 nanometres

b) Draw lines to match each nanoparticle with how it is made.

nanoparticle | how it is made
seaspray | by scientists
soot | by nature
silver nanoparticles | by accident

c) Nanoparticles are sometimes added to the plastic in tennis rackets. How do the nanoparticles make the plastic better? Give **one** way.

....

Q2 Why are people **worried** about using products that have **nanoparticles** in? Tick the box next to the right reason.

☐ We know that all nanoparticles are harmful to human health.

☐ We don't how nanoparticles affect the body.

☐ We don't know if nanoparticles really exist.

Q3 Complete the sentences below by circling the correct word(s) in each pair.

a) Nanoparticles **can** / **can't** be made in labs by scientists.

b) When fuels are burnt, **silver** / **soot** nanoparticles are made.

c) Silver nanoparticles **can** / **can't** help to kill bacteria.

d) Silver nanoparticles are used in **bandages** / **golf clubs**.

Module C2 — Material Choices

Mixed Questions — Module C2

Q1 Tick the right boxes to say if the following are **synthetic** materials or made from **living things**.

Synthetic means made by humans.

                        Natural   Synthetic

a) wool   ☐ ☐
b) nylon   ☐ ☐
c) silk   ☐ ☐
d) cotton   ☐ ☐
e) paper   ☐ ☐
f) PVC   ☐ ☐

Q2 Different materials are good at different things.

a) Why is rubber good for making car tyres? Circle **two** answers.

   it's shiny   it's mouldable   it's strong   it's stiff

b) Why is polypropene good for making kettles? Circle **two** answers.

Just think about what kind of things a kettle needs.

   it only lasts a short time   it's waterproof   it's bendy   it has a high melting point

Q3 **Crude oil** can be separated into **fractions**.

a) What is the method of separating crude oil into fractions called? Circle the right method.

        polymerisation   fractional distillation

b) Most crude oil is used to make fuel.
Name **one** other thing that crude oil fractions can be used for.

....

Petrol is made of **shorter** hydrocarbons than diesel.
Complete the sentences below by circling the correct word in each pair.

c) Long diesel molecules have **more / less** forces holding them together than short petrol molecules.

d) Petrol has shorter molecules than diesel so it has a **higher / lower** boiling point.

Module C2 — Material Choices

Mixed Questions — Module C2

Q4 Complete the table by picking a **material** from the list below to use for each product. You can only use each material **once**.

stainless steel   cotton   oak   glass   silver nanoparticles

Product	Material
Frying pan	
Window	
Surgical masks	
Cushion cover	
Bookcase	

Q5 Nigel has **two rulers** made from **different plastics**. He tries to **bend** them and then he **heats** them. His results are shown in the table.

	RESULT ON BENDING	RESULT ON HEATING
Ruler 1	Ruler bends easily and springs back into shape	Ruler becomes soft and then melts
Ruler 2	Ruler snaps in two	Ruler doesn't get soft

a) Which ruler is **stiffer**?

....

b) Which ruler has the **lowest melting point**?

....

Q6 Add the labels from the box to the diagram below.

polymer   monomers

a) ....   b) ....

Module C2 — Material Choices

Module C3 — Chemicals in Our Lives

Tectonic Plates

Q1 Are these sentences **true** or **false**? Tick the right boxes.

		True	False
a)	The Earth is made of just one layer.	☐	☐
b)	The Earth's crust is broken up into pieces called tectonic plates.	☐	☐
c)	Tectonic plates move around very quickly.	☐	☐
d)	The crust that makes up Britain has stayed very still on the surface of the Earth.	☐	☐

Q2 Use the words below to fill in the gaps in the sentences.

clues	tectonic plates	crust	magnetised

In some places, new .... is pushed up between tectonic plates.

This new crust is ....

Scientists look at the rock to work out how the .... have moved.

The magnetic rock gives them ....

Q3 a) What can scientists look at to tell them about the **Earth's history**? Tick the answer.

- ☐ trees
- ☐ animals
- ☐ rocks
- ☐ lakes

b) Three rocks (A, B and C) are described below.
Draw lines to join up the rocks with where they were made.

A. Has ripples on the surface

B. Contains shells

C. Contains an animal fossil

The rock was made underwater.

The rock was made on land.

Resources in the Earth's Crust

Q1 Circle the right words in the sentences.

a) Natural materials we can use are called **products / resources**.

b) Factories for making chemicals are usually built **near to / far away from** the resources.

c) There's a chemical industry in the **north-west / south-west** of England because there's limestone, salt and coal nearby.

Q2 Are these sentences **true** or **false**? Tick the right boxes.

	True	False
a) Seas are made of salt water.	☐	☐
b) All of the salt evaporated from some old seas.	☐	☐
c) Water evaporated from some old seas and the salt was left behind.	☐	☐

Q3 Draw lines to match up each word with its meaning.

evaporation — The wearing away of rocks by wind.

erosion — When a liquid changes to a gas.

Q4 Circle the right word in the sentence below.

Coal can be made when the pressure and temperature are **low / high**.

Q5 a) Write numbers in the boxes to put the sentences in the right order. One has been done for you.

[1] Sediment is made from shells and bones of sea creatures.

[ ] The weight pressing down turns the layers at the bottom into rock.

[ ] Layers of sediment get buried under more layers.

[ ] It's also made when the wind wears away rocks.

b) Name **one** sedimentary rock.

....

Module C3 — Chemicals in Our Lives

Salt

Q1 **Solution mining** is a way of getting salt out of the ground.

a) Labels A, B and C describe the different stages of solution mining.
Put the letters in the boxes to show what's happening in the diagram.

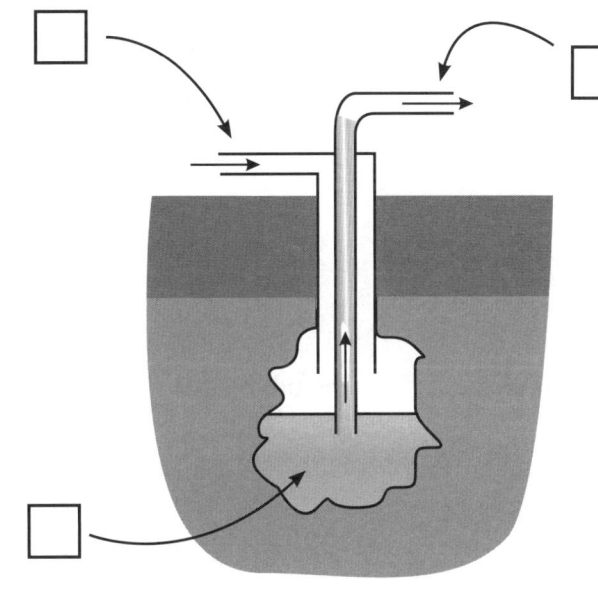

A   Pipes bring the salt water up to the surface.

B   Water is pumped into the salt deposit.

C   The water dissolves the salt.

b) Give **one** other way that you can get salt out of the ground.

....

c) Give **one** use for salt.

....

Q2 Why can mining salt be bad for the **environment**? Circle **two** answers.

Land above the old mines can collapse.

Mining causes pollution.

The salt isn't very useful.

Mining leaves too much salt in the ground.

Q3 You can get **salt** from **the sea**.
Write 1, 2 and 3 in the boxes to put the sentences in the right order.

☐ The water evaporates.

☐ The salt is left behind.

☐ Seawater is put in tanks and left in the sun.

Module C3 — Chemicals in Our Lives

Salt in the Food Industry

Q1 Why might salt be added to food? Tick **two** boxes.

- [ ] To preserve the food.
- [ ] To add colour.
- [ ] To improve the flavour.
- [ ] To help mix foods.

Food that's preserved lasts longer.

Q2 Which health problems could be caused by eating **too much salt**? Circle **three** answers.

high blood pressure   Parkinson's disease   mouth cancer

osteoporosis   strokes   glandular fever

Q3 The **food label** below is from a packet of bacon.

NUTRITIONAL INFORMATION	per packet	per 100 g
FAT	12.0 g	16.8 g
PROTEIN	3.2 g	4.5 g
SALT	0.8 g	1.2 g

a) How much salt is in the packet? Circle the answer.

1.2 g   12.0 g   0.8 g   3.2 g

b) Bob eats the packet of bacon. He also eats a bag of popcorn that has 4 g of salt. How much salt has he eaten in total?

....

Q4 The **Department of Health** and the **Department for Environment, Food and Rural Affairs** give advice on food safety. What are their jobs? Tick **two** boxes.

- [ ] Telling people about how food affects their health.
- [ ] Checking that people eat enough bananas.
- [ ] Checking that supermarkets sell enough food.
- [ ] Checking that chemicals used in food are safe.

Module C3 — Chemicals in Our Lives

Electrolysis of Salt Solution

Q1 What happens in **electrolysis**? Tick the right box.

An electric current is passed through a solution. ☐

Electricity splits a solid up. ☐

A salt is made using an electric current. ☐

Q2 You can get **chlorine** using electrolysis. What do you pass the electric current through? Circle the answer.

solid salt   sodium hydroxide   hydrogen

water   salt solution

Q3 Which chemical is used for the things in the list below? Tick the right boxes. One has been done for you.

	Chlorine	Hydrogen	Sodium hydroxide
a) Used in oven cleaner	☐	☐	✓
b) Used to kill bacteria	☐	☐	☐
c) Used to make ammonia	☐	☐	☐
d) Used to make soap	☐	☐	☐
e) Used to make margarine	☐	☐	☐

Q4 Use the words below to fill in the gaps in the sentences.

fossil fuels   environment   carbon dioxide   energy

Electrolysis needs a lot of ....

This comes from burning ....

This releases pollutants such as .... into the atmosphere.

This can damage the ....

Module C3 — Chemicals in Our Lives

Chlorination

Q1 What is **chlorination**? Tick the right box.

☐ Adding chlorine to water.

☐ Removing chlorine from water.

Q2 Why is chlorine added to water? Circle **one** reason.

It filters water.   It kills bacteria.

It reacts to make harmful chemicals.   It makes water freeze.

Q3 Use a word from the box to fill in the missing word in the sentence below.

> carbon dioxide   water   oxygen

Hydrogen chloride and .... react to make chlorine.

Q4 The graph shows how the number of people getting a disease has changed.

a) What happened when chlorination was started? Tick the right box.

☐ The number of people getting the disease went up.

☐ The number of people getting the disease went down.

☐ The number of people getting the disease didn't change.

b) Give **one** problem with using chlorine to treat water.

....

Module C3 — Chemicals in Our Lives

Alkalis

Q1 a) Which equation shows the reaction between an **acid** and an **alkali**? Circle the answer.

| acid + alkali → salt + oxygen | acid + alkali → salt + sulfur dioxide |

| acid + alkali → carbon dioxide + water | acid + alkali → salt + water |

b) What type of reaction is this? Circle the answer.

electrolysis   neutralisation   chlorination

Q2 Tick **four** things that alkalis are used for.

☐ Turning fats and oils into soap.   ☐ Helping dyes stick to cloth.
☐ Making margarine.   ☐ Making acidic soil neutral.
☐ Making glass.   ☐ Making bleach.

Q3 Name **two** things that were used as alkalis **in the past**.

1. ....
2. ....

Q4 Circle the right word in the sentence below.

When industry became important in Britain, **more** / **less** alkalis were needed.

Q5 a) What was used to make **alkalis** in the **19th Century**? Circle the answer.

chlorine and water   limestone and salt

hydrogen and salt   limestone and chlorine

b) Circle the right words in the sentences to show the problems with this reaction.

It released large amounts of **hydrogen chloride** / **sulfur dioxide** into the air.

It also produced a lot of **liquid** / **solid** waste.

Module C3 — Chemicals in Our Lives

Impacts of Chemical Production

Q1 Are these sentences **true** or **false**? Tick the right boxes.   True False
   a) Chemicals can't be used to make many things.   ☐ ☐
   b) Chemicals can't always be tested as much as we'd like.   ☐ ☐
   c) We don't know if some chemicals could harm the environment.   ☐ ☐
   d) We know that chemicals can't harm people's health.   ☐ ☐

Q2 a) What type of material is **PVC**? Tick the correct answer.

   ☐ monomer   ☐ plasticiser   ☐ polymer

   b) What is PVC made of? Circle the **three** answers.

   carbon   phosphorus   hydrogen   chlorine   vanadium   oxygen

Q3 Are these sentences **true** or **false**? Tick the right boxes.   True False
   a) Plasticisers are not harmful.   ☐ ☐
   b) Plasticisers can leak out of PVC and into water nearby.   ☐ ☐
   c) Plasticisers can build up in animals and end up being eaten by humans.   ☐ ☐

Q4 Look at the **food chain** below.

   Algae → Water louse → Dragonfly nymph → Water shrew → Kestrel

   A chemical has got into the lake where the algae live.

   a) Could the kestrel be harmed by the chemical? Circle the answer.

   yes   no

   b) What is the reason for your answer to **(a)**? Tick the right box.

   ☐ The kestrel doesn't eat the algae so it won't be harmed.
   ☐ The chemical can be passed along the food chain to the kestrel.
   ☐ The kestrel eats the algae and is harmed by the chemical.

Module C3 — Chemicals in Our Lives

Life Cycle Assessments

Q1 What is a life cycle assessment? Tick the right box.

☐ A life cycle assessment looks at how easy it is to get rid of a product.

☐ A life cycle assessment looks at how easy it is to make a product.

☐ A life cycle assessment looks at all the stages in the life of a product.

Q2 There are different **stages** in the **life of a product**.
Write 1, 2, 3 and 4 in the boxes to put the stages in the right order.

☐ Making the product.

☐ Getting rid of the product.

☐ Using the product.

☐ Making the material.

Q3 What **three** things do scientists need to look at in **each stage** of a product's life? Circle three answers.

What resources (materials) are used.

Whether the environment is damaged.

Whether people like the colour of the product.

How much energy is used or made.

How much the product will cost to buy.

Q4 Are these sentences **true** or **false**? Tick the right boxes. True False

a) Once a product is made it can't harm the environment any more. ☐ ☐

b) Energy is usually used to make a product. ☐ ☐

c) Making a product can cause a lot of pollution. ☐ ☐

d) Some waste materials can be recycled instead of being thrown away. ☐ ☐

e) Making a product doesn't use up resources. ☐ ☐

Module C3 — Chemicals in Our Lives

Life Cycle Assessments

Q5 a) **Fossil fuels** are being used to power a factory. Give **one** problem with this.

....

b) How can the amount of waste that the factory makes be **reduced**?
Tick the right box.

☐ The waste can be recycled and used again.

☐ The waste can be buried.

☐ More product can be made.

Q6 Helen is looking at the life cycle assessment for two CD racks.
One is **metal**. The other is **plastic**.

Which **stage** of the life cycle assessment would be the **same** for both of the racks? Circle the answer.

Making the material   Getting rid of the product   Using the product

Q7 Harry's factory is making **metal spoons**.
Draw lines to join the processes to the stage of the life cycle assessment.

Making the metal into spoons   Making the material

Getting the metal from metal ore   Getting rid of the product

Putting the spoons in the bin   Using the product

People using the spoons at home   Making the product

Q8 Compare a plastic drinks bottle with a metal toaster.

a) Which product will last **longest**? Circle the answer.
plastic drinks bottle   metal toaster

b) Which product will **cost** more to make? Circle the answer.
plastic drinks bottle   metal toaster

c) Which product is more likely to be **recycled**? Circle the answer.
plastic drinks bottle   metal toaster

Module C3 — Chemicals in Our Lives

Mixed Questions — Module C3

Q1 Are these sentences **true** or **false**? Tick the right boxes.

                                                                                                          True False

a) The Earth is made up of different layers.

b) The rocks in Britain were made in the climate Britain has now.

c) The crust that makes up Britain has moved over the surface of the Earth.

d) The crust is made of one big tectonic plate.

e) Magnetic rocks can give scientists clues about how tectonic plates have moved.

Q2 Sedimentary rock is made from **sediment**. Name **two** ways that sediment is made.

1. ....

2. ....

Q3 a) The first way of making **alkalis** used limestone.
What was the limestone reacted with? Circle the answer.

        carbon dioxide   oxygen   chlorine   salt   hydrogen

b) Making alkalis this way made a lot of **solid waste**. Why was this a problem?

....

Q4 Use the words in the box to fill in the **neutralisation** reaction.

                salt   alkali   water

acid + ... ⟹ .... + ...

Q5 Draw lines to join chlorine, hydrogen and sodium hydroxide to the products that they're used for.

    bleach   Chlorine   margarine

    soap   Hydrogen   disinfectant

    ammonia   Sodium hydroxide   oven cleaner

Some products may be made from more than one thing.

Module C3 — Chemicals in Our Lives

Mixed Questions — Module C3

Q6 Are these sentences **true** or **false**? Tick the right boxes.

    True False

a) Salt made by mining is used to grit roads. ☐ ☐

b) Salt can be mined by pumping mud into salt deposits. ☐ ☐

c) Mining doesn't use much energy. ☐ ☐

d) The salt made by solution mining is used for table salt and making chemicals. ☐ ☐

Q7 Circle the right words in the sentences below.

a) Salt is added to food to make its **texture** / **flavour** better.

b) Eating too much salt can cause **high** / **low** blood pressure.

c) Eating less salt **increases** / **decreases** your risk of having a stroke.

d) **Electrolysis** / **Solution mining** is used to split salt solution into chlorine, sodium hydroxide and hydrogen.

Q8 a) Name a government department that gives advice on **food safety**.

....

b) This department looks at the health risks of different foods. What is this called? Tick the right box.

☐ chemical testing

☐ risk assessment

☐ life cycle assessment

Q9 PVC is used to make pipes. Draw lines to match up the **stage** of PVC's life with the **environmental problem** it could cause.

Using the pipes   Uses up fossil fuels and makes waste.

Making the pipes   Plasticisers may leak out into water nearby.

Getting rid of the pipes   If they're burnt, there could be air pollution.

Module C3 — Chemicals in Our Lives

Module P1 — The Earth in the Universe

The Solar System

Q1 Label the diagram by filling in the gaps. Use the words in the box below.

> Sun   planet   asteroid   comet

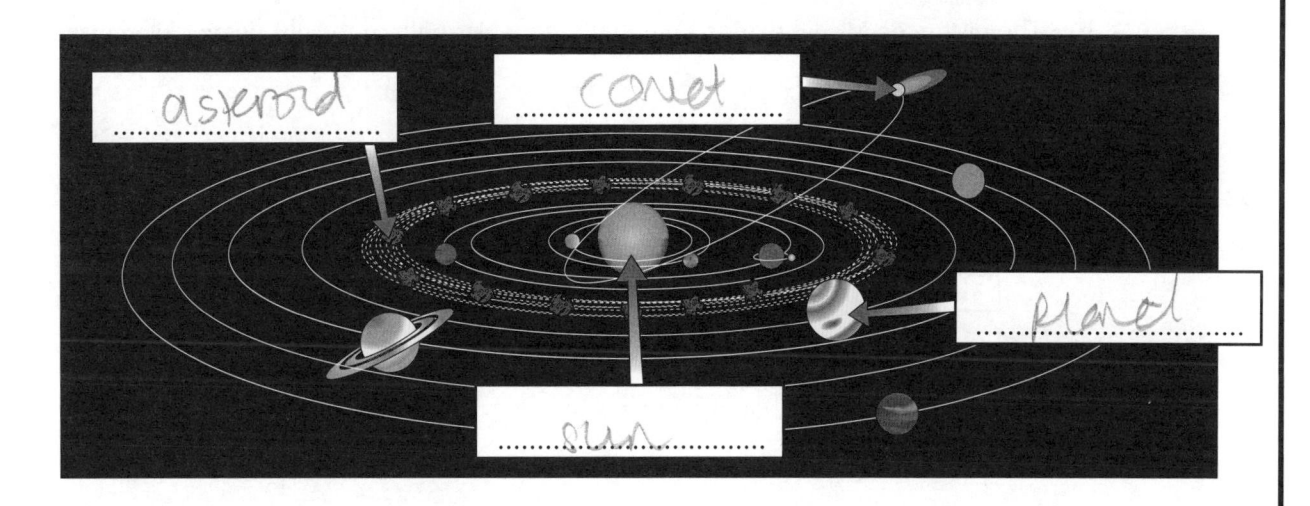

- asteroid
- comet
- planet
- sun

Q2 Circle the right words in the sentences below.

a) There are **eight** / **nine** planets in the Solar System. *[eight circled]*

b) Planets orbit the **Sun** / **Moon**. *[Sun circled]*

c) Moons orbit the **Sun** / **planets**. *[planets circled]*

d) The Solar System is about **5** / **10** thousand million years old. *[5 circled]*

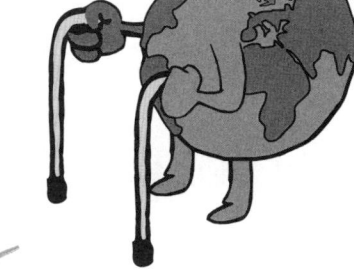

Q3 Are these sentences **true** or **false**? Tick the boxes.

	True	False
a) The Solar System started as a cloud of asteroids.		✓
b) Hydrogen atoms can join to make helium in stars.	✓	
c) Heavy elements can be made in stars.	✓	

Q4 What is the name of the process that gives out **heat** and **light energy** in stars? Circle your answer.

asteroid   **fusion** *[circled]*   orbiting   Big Bang

Beyond the Solar System

Q1 Circle the right words to complete the sentences below.

a) Light travels really **slowly** / **quickly** in space.

b) The distances in space are so big that we measure them in **light years** / **kilometres**.

Q2 What is a **light year**? Tick the box next to the answer.

☐ The amount of light that reaches Earth in a year.
☐ The speed that light waves move.
☑ The distance that light travels in a year.
☐ The amount of time it takes light from the Sun to reach the Earth.

Q3 Draw lines to match the object to its age.

You need to use one of the boxes twice.

Earth — 5000 million years
Universe — 14 000 million years
Sun —

Q4 Put the following options in order of **smallest to largest**. Two have been done for you.

Options: diameter of the Solar System, diameter of the Milky Way, ~~diameter of the Earth~~, diameter of the Sun, distance between galaxies

SMALLEST — diameter of the Earth
diameter of sun
diameter of solar system
diameter of the Milky Way
LARGEST — distance between galaxies

Diameter is the distance from one side to the other.

Module P1 — The Earth in the Universe

Looking Into Space

Q1 How can you **measure** the **distance** to a **star**? Circle two answers.

A — using parallax

B — using fusion

C — by counting how many planets it has

D — by looking at its brightness

Q2 a) Circle the right word to complete the sentence below.

The amount of light a star gives out is called its **parallax** / **brightness**.

b) Which two things affect how bright a star looks from Earth? Tick **two** boxes.

- How far away from Earth the star is. ☐
- How long it takes light from the star to reach Earth. ☐
- How bright the star actually is. ☐
- The size of the star. ☐

c) What effect does the atmosphere have on light from space? Circle your answer.

It increases the amount of light from space.

It doesn't affect the amount of light from space.

It absorbs some of the light from space.

d) How does light pollution affect how easy it is to see stars? Circle your answer.

It makes it easier to see stars.

It doesn't affect how easy it is to see stars.

It makes it harder to see stars.

Q3 Why do we see stars as they were **in the past**? Tick the box next to the answer.

☐ The light from stars travels very slowly in space.
☐ Stars are always moving further away from the Earth.
☐ The light from stars has to travel a very long way to reach the Earth.
☐ The Earth is orbiting the Sun a lot faster than the other stars.

Module P1 — The Earth in the Universe

The Life of the Universe

Q1 Which of the following sentences are **true**? Tick two answers.

- The Earth is getting smaller. ☐
- Other galaxies are moving away from us. ☑
- The Universe is getting bigger. ☑
- The Universe was made by a volcanic eruption. ☐
- The Moon is getting bigger. ☐

Q2 Some scientists think the Universe **began** with an **explosion**.

a) What name is given to this explosion?

.... Big Bang ....

b) How many **years** ago do scientists think that this explosion happened? Circle your answer.

14 million   17 million   **(14 000 million)**   17 000 million

c) Number the boxes 1-3 to show how the Universe was made.

- There was a large explosion. [2]
- The material started spreading out and the Universe got bigger. [3]
- All of the material in the Universe was squashed into a tiny space. [1]

Q3 It's hard for scientists to be sure if and when the Universe will end. Why is this? Circle **two** answers.

- They don't know how much friction is in the Universe.
- (It's hard to measure the distances between objects in space.)
- (It's hard to know how things move in space.)
- They don't know the temperature of the Universe.

Module P1 — The Earth in the Universe

The Changing Earth

Q1 Draw lines to match the **process** to its **description**.

PROCESS | DESCRIPTION

- Folding — Sediment is crushed together under the sea. This makes new rock.
- Erosion — Rocks are broken into bits over a long time.
- Sedimentation — Rocks are squeezed together so much that they fold.

Q2 Are these sentences **true** or **false**? Tick the boxes. True False

a) Without new rock, continents would be worn down and the Earth would be smooth. ☐ ☐

b) Fossils are made when rocks are eroded. ☐ ☐

c) Changes in rocks can be used to show how the Sun has changed. ☐ ☐

Q3 The oldest rocks on Earth are about **4000 million years old**. What does this tell us? Tick the box next to the answer.

☐ All rocks were formed 4000 million years ago.
☐ The Earth is at least 4000 million years old.
☐ The Solar System is less than 4000 million years old.
☐ The Earth was much bigger 4000 million years ago.

Q4 a) What are **fossils**?

....

b) Fossils are found inside rocks. What does this tell us about rocks? Circle your answer.

| They have holes for animals to crawl into. | They are soft. | New rock has been made over time. |

Module P1 — The Earth in the Universe

Wegener's Theory of Continental Drift

Q1 Below is a letter that **Wegener** might have written. Use the words in the box below to fill in the gaps.

> fossils   continents
> continental drift   joined together

Dear Mr Heinz,

I am writing to tell you about my idea of ....

I can explain why there are matching .... in different continents. I think that millions of years ago the continents were

.... The Earth is made of chunks that have split apart. When these moved apart they took the

.... with them.

From,

wegener :)

Q2 Wegener had **reasons** for his idea.

Tick **two** boxes to show what his reasons were.

He found lines in the ground that showed where the continents had split apart.	☐
He found matching fossils in different continents.	☐
He could still see the glue from where the continents were once joined together.	☐
He saw that the continents would fit together like a jigsaw.	☐

Q3 Below are two different ideas about how **mountains** were made.

Tick the box next to Wegener's idea.

☐ The Earth shrunk and crinkled as it cooled down. This made the mountains.

☐ Mountains were made when parts of the Earth crashed together.

Module P1 — The Earth in the Universe

Wegener's Theory of Continental Drift

Q4 Wegener used the layers in rock to back up his theory.

a) Circle the two continents that may have been joined together.

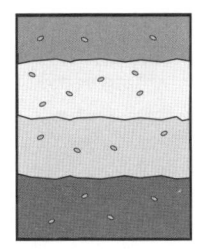

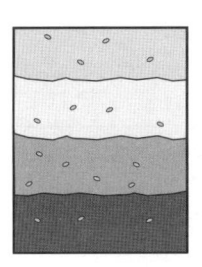

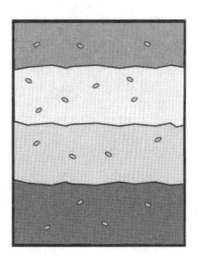

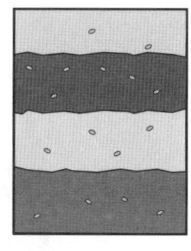

    Continent A   Continent B   Continent C   Continent D

b) Explain your answer to part **a)**.

....

Q5 Are these sentences **true** or **false**? Tick the boxes.

                                                                                                  True False

a) Wegener found different fossils on every continent.

b) Wegener's theory explained how mountain building happens.

Q6 Why did other scientists not believe Wegener's theory at first? Circle **four** answers.

- Wegener forgot to use proof from fossils in his theory.
- Wegener was too young to be making theories.
- Wegener wasn't a geologist.
- Other people had simpler ideas and explanations.
- Wegener didn't have much evidence that he was right.
- No one could see that the continents were moving.

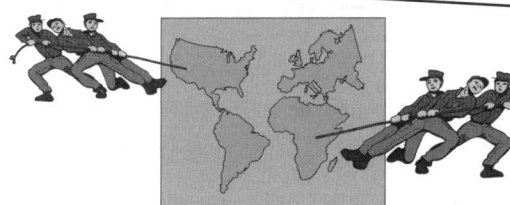

Q7 Circle the right words in the sentences below.

Scientists found that the sea floor was **getting smaller / spreading apart**.

This meant that Wegener's theory was **wrong / right**.

Module P1 — The Earth in the Universe

The Structure of the Earth

Q1 The diagram shows the Earth's structure. Label the **crust**, **core** and **mantle**.

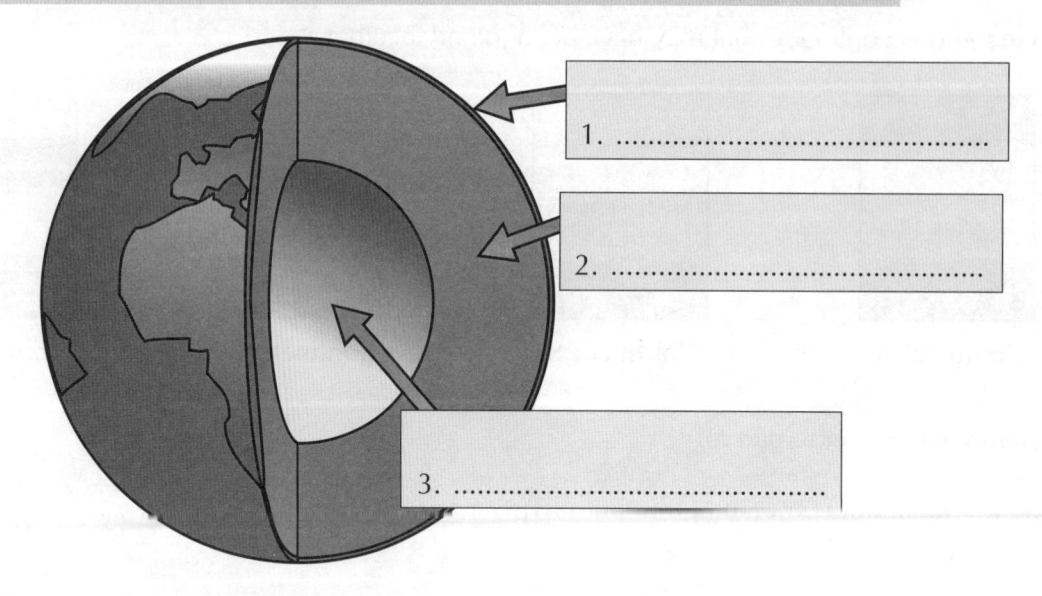

1. ....

2. ....

3. ....

Q2 Circle the right word in the sentences below.

In the mantle there are **convection** / **radiation** currents.

These cause the mantle to **break up** / **flow**.

This also causes the **sea floor** / **core** to spread.

Q3 The map on the left shows where most of the world's **earthquakes** take place. The map on the right shows the **tectonic plates**.

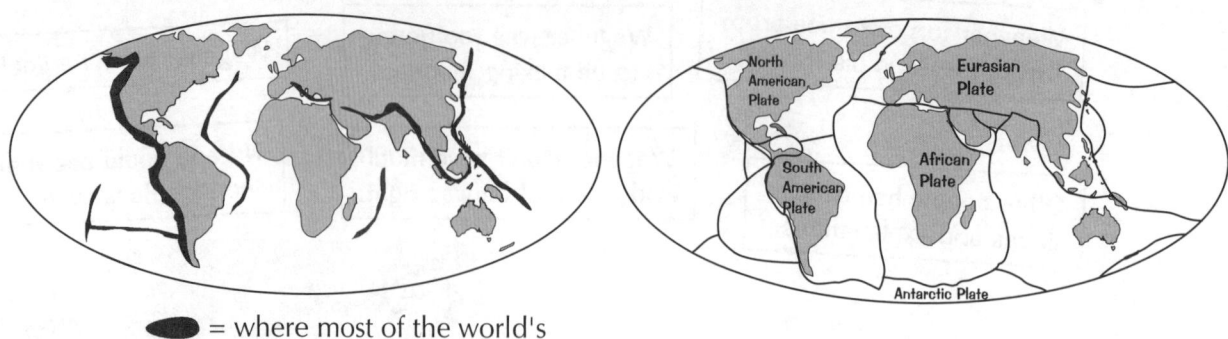

⬛ = where most of the world's earthquakes take place

Compare the two maps. What do they tell you about where earthquakes happen? Circle the answer.

Earthquakes never happen where tectonic plates meet.

Most earthquakes happen where tectonic plates meet.

Earthquakes happen when things crash into the Earth.

Module P1 — The Earth in the Universe

Seismic Waves

Q1 Circle the right word in the sentences below.

Earthquakes / Mountains can cause waves.

These are called EM / seismic waves.

Q2 Are the following sentences about **P-waves**, **S-waves** or **both**? Tick the boxes.

One has been done for you.

	P-wave	S-wave
This type of wave can be caused by an earthquake.	✓	✓
a) This type of wave does not pass through liquids.	☐	✓
b) This type of wave can pass through liquids and solids.	✓	☐
c) This type of wave can travel through the mantle.	✓	✓
d) This type of wave can travel through the Earth's core.	✓	☐

Q3 Circle the letter next to the **one** sentence that is **true**.

A   P-waves can only travel a few metres.

B   P-waves cannot be picked up by instruments on the Earth's surface.

C   S-waves can only travel through solids.   T

D   P-waves can only travel through liquids.

Q4 A scientist measures the waves from an **earthquake**. The scientist is on the **other side** of the world to the earthquake.

a) What type of wave can the scientist pick up?

.... P ....

b) What does this tell the scientist? Circle your answer.

(The waves can pass through the core.)

The waves can not pass through the core.

There are tectonic plates on the core.

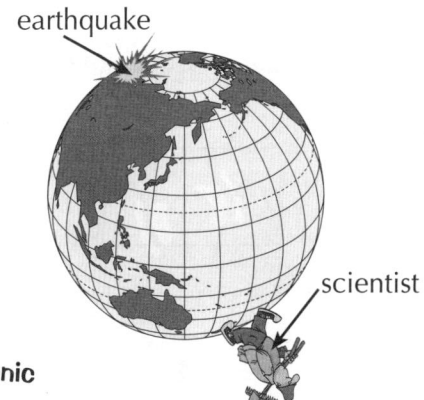

Module P1 — The Earth in the Universe

… 84

Waves — The Basics

Q1 Circle the right word in the sentence below.

> Waves transfer **energy** / **matter** from one place to another.

Q2 Label the different parts of the wave using the words below.

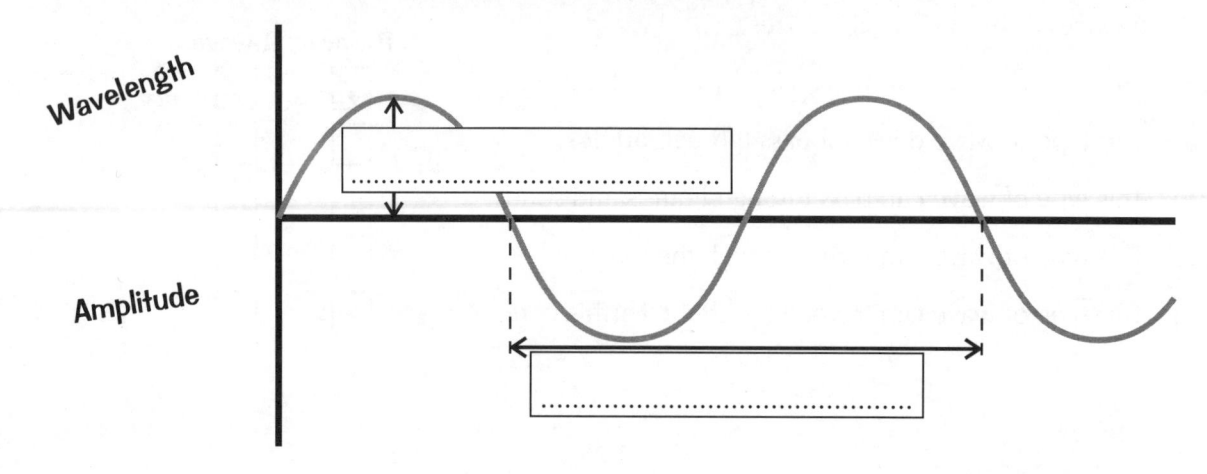

Wavelength

Amplitude

Q3 Complete the sentences below by circling the right word.

a) Frequency is the number of **waves** / **amplitudes** per second.

b) Frequency is measured in **Hz** / **mm**.

c) The **wavelength** / **amplitude** is the length of a full cycle of a wave.

Q4 Diagrams A, B and C show different waves.

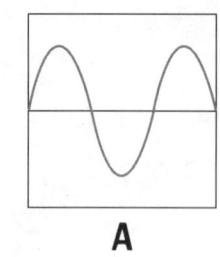

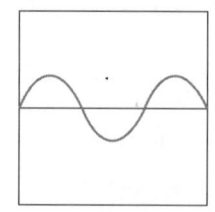

A   B   C

a) Which two diagrams show waves with the same **amplitude**? ...A... and ...B...

b) Which two diagrams show waves with the same **wavelength**? ...A... and ...C...

Module P1 — The Earth in the Universe

Waves — The Basics

Example: A wave has a wavelength of **2 m** and a frequency of **125 Hz**.
Calculate the **speed** of the wave. Give the correct units in your answer.

wave speed = frequency × wavelength ← Write out the equation for wave speed.

wave speed = 125 Hz × 2 m = 250 m/s ← Don't forget to write the correct units.

Plug the numbers in. Work out the answer with a calculator.

Q5 A **sound wave** has a wavelength of **4 m** and a frequency of **85 Hz**.

wave speed = frequency × wavelength

Calculate the **speed** of the sound wave. Give the correct units in your answer.

4 × 85

Q6 A **water wave** has a frequency of **2.5 Hz** and a wavelength of **1.2 m**.

Tick the box to show the **speed** of the water wave.

3 m/s ☐   2.1 m/s ☐   0.5 m/s ☐   3.7 Hz ☐

2.5 × 1.2

Q7 Tick the box next to the sentence that is about a **transverse** wave.

☑ The vibrations are at 90° to the way the wave is going.

☐ The vibrations move the same way as the wave is going.

Q8 The diagrams show **two ways** to make waves on a **slinky** spring.

Which diagram shows a **transverse** wave, and which one shows a **longitudinal** wave?

Transverse: ......long............
Longitudinal: ......Transverse............

① ②

Module P1 — The Earth in the Universe

Mixed Questions — Module P1

Q1 Circle the **true** sentence.

A — The Moon orbits comets.   C — The Milky Way orbits the Sun.

B — There are eight planets that orbit the Sun.

Q2 Choose from the words below to complete the sentences.

radiation	atmosphere	pollution

Scientists use .... coming from space to learn more about stars.

The Earth's .... absorbs some light before it can reach us on Earth.

Light .... makes it hard to see dim objects.

Q3 **Seismic waves** can travel on the surface and inside the Earth.

a) What is the Earth's crust? Tick the answer.

The outer layer we live on. ☐

The layer in the middle of the Earth. ☐

The layer of clouds in the atmosphere. ☐

The centre of the earth. ☐

b) What causes seismic waves?

....

c) Which type of seismic wave can pass through the liquid centre of the Earth? Circle the answer.

P-waves   S-waves

Module P1 — The Earth in the Universe

Mixed Questions — Module P1

Q4 a) Draw lines to match the statement to the wave.

- Has the largest amplitude
- Has the smallest amplitude
- Has the shortest wavelength

A, B, C

b) How fast do **light waves** travel in space? Circle your answer.

300 000 km/s   30 000 km/s   30 km/s   300 000 000 km/s

Q5 A radio wave has a wavelength of **1500 m** and a frequency of **200 000 Hz**.

Calculate the **speed** of the radio wave.

wave speed = frequency × wavelength

....

.... m/s

Q6 Fill in the gaps to complete the sentences. Choose from the words below each sentence.

a) Erosion causes rock to be ....

melted   broken into bits   folded

b) Bits of eroded rock get washed into the sea and settle as ....

sediment   fossils   lava

c) .... of rocks happens when rocks are squeezed together so much they fold.

Erosion   Sedimentation   Folding

d) .... are evidence for Wegener's theory of continental drift.

Comets   Fossils   P-waves

Module P1 — The Earth in the Universe

Electromagnetic Radiation

Q1 Complete the **electromagnetic spectrum** below. Use the words from the list.

infrared   X-rays   microwaves   ultraviolet

| radio waves | microwaves | infrared | light | ultraviolet | X-rays | gamma rays |

Lowest frequency ———————————→ Highest frequency

Q2 a) Which sort of electromagnetic radiation has the **highest energy photons**? Circle the answer.

radio waves   **(gamma rays)**

Look at the electromagnetic spectrum in Q1 to help you with question 2.

b) Which sort of electromagnetic radiation has the **lowest energy photons**? Circle the answer.

(radio waves)   light waves

c) Which sort of electromagnetic radiation has the **higher frequency**? Circle the answer.

microwaves   **(ultraviolet)**

d) Which sort of electromagnetic radiation has the **lower frequency**? Circle the answer.

(infrared)   X-rays

Q3 Are these sentences **true** or **false**? Tick the boxes.

		True	False
a)	Photons are packets of energy.	✓	
b)	Light is the only electromagnetic radiation you can see.	✓	✓
c)	High frequency waves have low energy photons.		✓
d)	The frequency of the waves decreases as you go along the spectrum from radio waves to gamma rays.		✓

Electromagnetic Radiation and Energy

Q1 Draw lines to match the words with their descriptions.

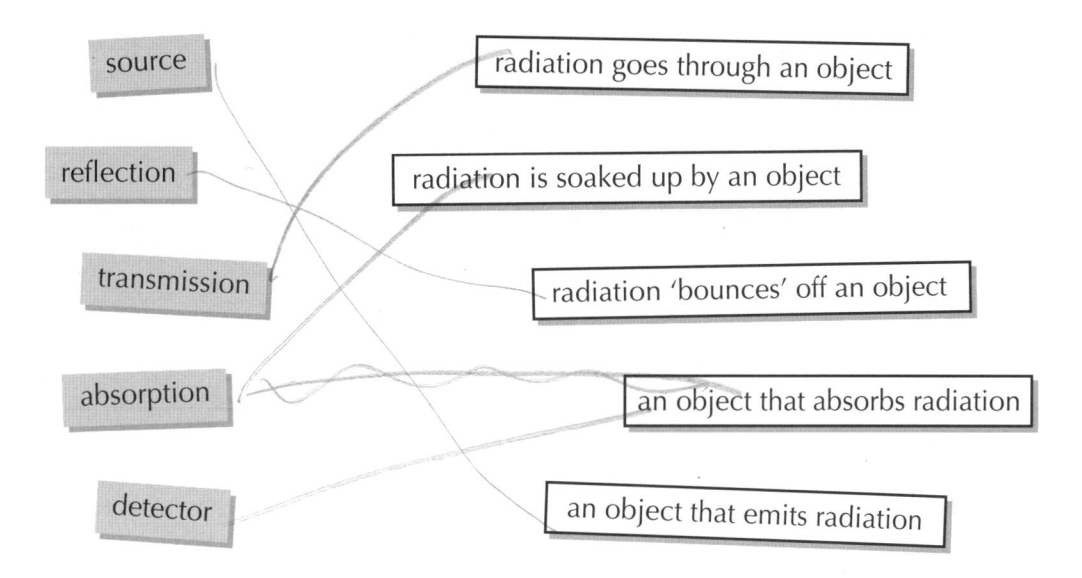

- source — an object that emits radiation
- reflection — radiation 'bounces' off an object
- transmission — radiation goes through an object
- absorption — radiation is soaked up by an object
- detector — an object that absorbs radiation

Q2 Circle the right words to complete the sentences.

Sources of electromagnetic radiation emit energy.

The total energy depends on the **(energy)** / length of the photons emitted by the source.

The total energy depends on the colour / **(number)** of photons emitted by the source.

Really **(hot)** / cold sources give off high frequency radiation.

Really hot / **(cold)** sources give off lower frequency radiation.

Q3 a) Circle the right word to complete the sentence.

The strength of radiation is how much **(energy)** / frequency hits a surface each second.

b) In the diagram below, Ed is stood much closer to a fire than Karen. Why does Ed feel warmer than Karen? Circle the answer.

(More photons reach Ed, so he absorbs more energy.)

Photons with higher energy reach Ed, so he absorbs more energy.

photons emitted by the fire

Module P2 — Radiation and Life

Ionising Radiation

Q1 Circle the right words to complete the sentences.

> Radioactive materials give off **radiation** / electricity all the time.
>
> Ionising radiation has **photons** / electrons with really high energies.
>
> If ionising radiation hits an atom or molecule it can knock off **an electron** / a photon.
>
> This makes an **ion** / X-ray.
>
> Ionising radiation can damage your clothes / **cells**.

Q2 Circle the **three** types of **ionising** radiation.

- ultraviolet (circled)
- visible light
- **gamma rays** (circled)
- microwaves (circled — incorrect)
- X-rays (circled)
- radio waves
- infrared

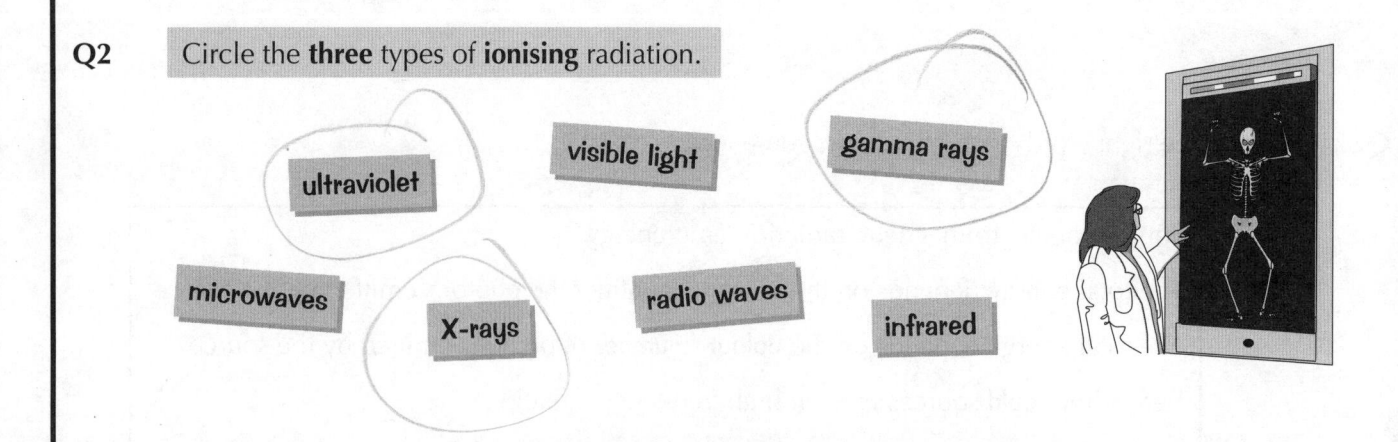

Q3 Add the labels below to the diagram to show **ionisation**.

molecule   radiation   ion   electron

BEFORE IONISATION — radiation, molecule

AFTER IONISATION — electron, ion

Module P2 — Radiation and Life

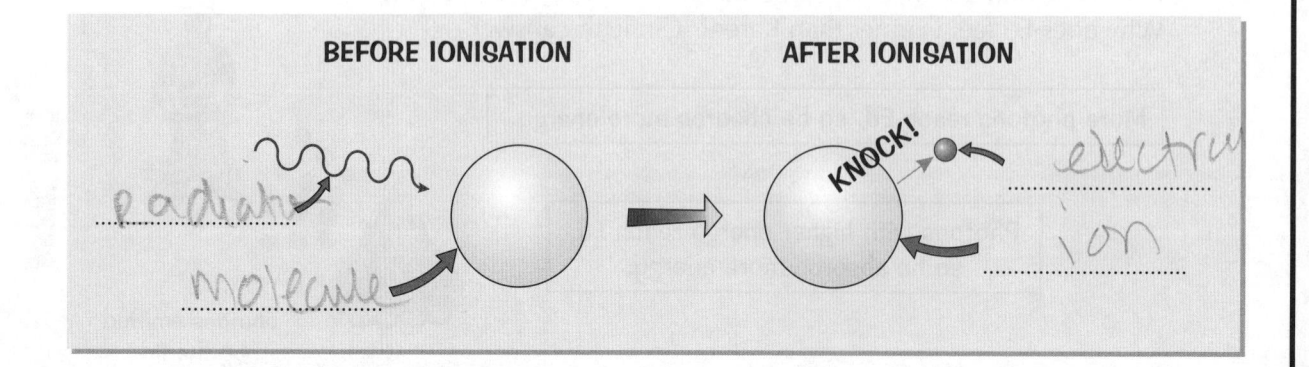

Ionising Radiation

Q4 Are these sentences **true** or **false**? Tick the right boxes.

		True	False
a)	Ionising radiation only damages your clothes and make up.	☐	✓
b)	Lots of ionising radiation can cause cell death.	✓	☐
c)	Lots of ionising radiation can cause cancer.	✓	☐

Q5 **X-rays** are used in hospitals.

a) Fill in the blanks using the words in the box below.

bones   flesh   pictures

Hospitals use X-rays to produce ...*pictures*... to see if a patient has any broken bones. X-rays cannot pass easily through dense materials like ...*bones*... and metal because they are absorbed by them. X-rays pass through ...*flesh*... more easily because it's less dense.

b) Circle **one** other use of X-rays.

Cooking food   Photocopying   **(Scanning bags at airports)**

Q6 The Sun emits **ultraviolet (UV)** radiation.

a) Complete the sentence by **underlining** the correct word.

Sunscreens can protect us from the Sun's rays by **absorbing** / <u>refracting</u> UV radiation.

b) Give **one** other way you can protect yourself from the **Sun's** UV radiation.

...*clothing*...

Module P2 — Radiation and Life

Microwaves

Q1 Circle the right words to complete the sentences below.

Microwave ovens **give out** / **transmit** microwaves.

The microwaves are **absorbed** / **reflected** by the water molecules in food.

The water molecules **break apart** / **heat up**. This heats up the food.

Q2 Are these sentences **true** or **false**? Tick the boxes.

		True	False
a)	No molecules in food absorb microwaves.		✓
b)	Microwave ovens can't stop microwaves getting out.	✓	✓
c)	Metal reflects and absorbs microwaves.	✓	

Q3 a) **Microwaves** can be **dangerous**. Tick the reason why.

☐ If cells in your body absorb microwaves they cool down.

☑ If cells in your body absorb microwaves they heat up.

b) Microwave ovens stop microwave radiation getting out. Which parts do this? Circle **two** answers.

the metal case   the turntable   the electric wires

the vent   the door screen

Q4 Circle the right words in the sentences below.

Some people are worried that mobile phones might be dangerous.

This is because **microwaves** / **mastwaves** carry calls between mobile phones and phone masts.

Some of this radiation is **absorbed** / **reflected** by your body.

There is **a lot of** / **not much** evidence that mobiles are dangerous.

Module P2 — Radiation and Life

Electromagnetic Radiation and the Atmosphere

Q1 Complete the sentences by circling the correct words.

a) The Sun emits **electromagnetic** / **ozone** radiation.

b) The Earth is surrounded by an atmosphere made of **gases** / **rocks**.

c) Some radiation from the Sun is absorbed by the Earth which **warms it up** / **cools it down**.

Q2 Tick **one** box next to a **greenhouse gas**.

nitrogen ☐   carbon dioxide ☐   oxygen ☐

Q3 The diagram below shows how the greenhouse effect keeps the Earth warm. Use the descriptions **A** to **C** to label the diagram. One has been done for you.

A Some of the radiation is reflected back to Earth by the greenhouse gases.

B The Earth gives out some of the heat radiation it absorbs.

C Some of this radiation is absorbed by greenhouse gases.

Q4 a) What type of radiation is absorbed by ozone? Circle the answer.

Infrared   Ultraviolet   Radio waves   Light

b) Which of the sentences below is true? Circle the answer.

The ozone layer protects life on Earth from harmful radiation.

The ozone layer harms life on Earth by releasing harmful radiation.

Module P2 — Radiation and Life

The Carbon Cycle

Q1 Add the labels to the diagram of the **carbon cycle**.

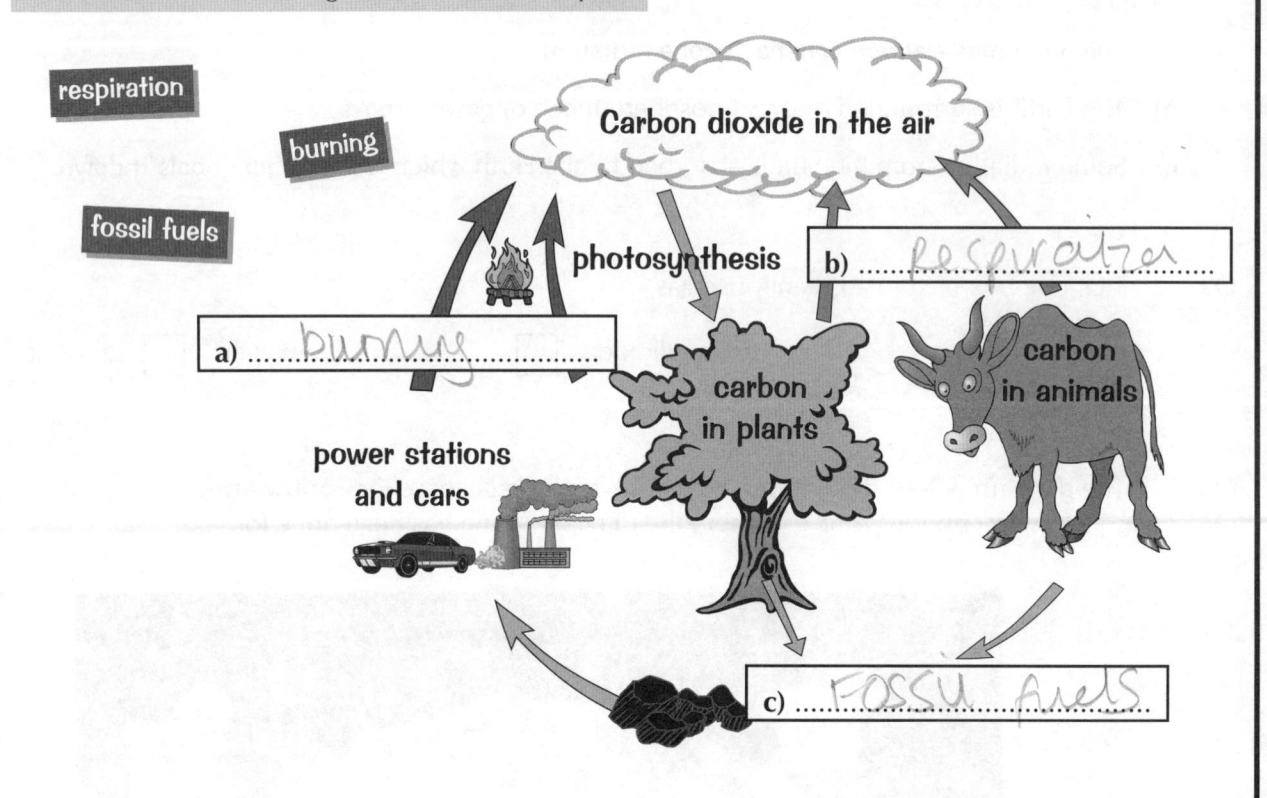

a) burning
b) respiration
c) fossil fuels

Q2 a) For thousands of years the amount of carbon dioxide in the Earth's atmosphere **stayed the same**. Why did it stay the same? Circle the letter next to the answer.

- A No carbon dioxide was added and no carbon dioxide was removed.
- **B** The amount of carbon dioxide taken from the air was the same as the amount of carbon dioxide added to the air.
- C The temperature was too low for photosynthesis.

b) Over the past 200 years, the amount of carbon dioxide has **increased**. Why has it increased? Tick **two** boxes.

- ✓ More trees are being cut down and burnt.
- ☐ More plants are photosynthesising.
- ✓ More fossil fuels are being burnt for energy.

Module P2 — Radiation and Life

Global Warming and Climate Change

Q1 Fill in the blanks with the words below.

carbon dioxide	greenhouse	temperatures

The amount of ......*carbon dioxide*...... in the atmosphere has increased.

This has upset the ......*greenhouse*...... effect. Because of this,

......*temperatures*...... have risen — this is global warming.

Q2 Are these sentences **true** or **false**? Tick the boxes.

		True	False
a)	Global temperatures are decreasing.		✓
b)	The amount of carbon dioxide in the atmosphere has been increasing.	✓	
c)	Global warming is caused by climate change.	✓	
d)	Global warming could never cause the sea level to rise.		✓
e)	Global warming can affect the weather.	✓	

Q3 Write the numbers 1-4 in the boxes below to show the order of the statements.

One has been done for you.

- [2] Warmer seas also cause ice to melt.
- [1] As the sea gets warmer it gets bigger.
- [4] This rising sea level could cause some places to flood.
- [3] This makes the sea level rise.

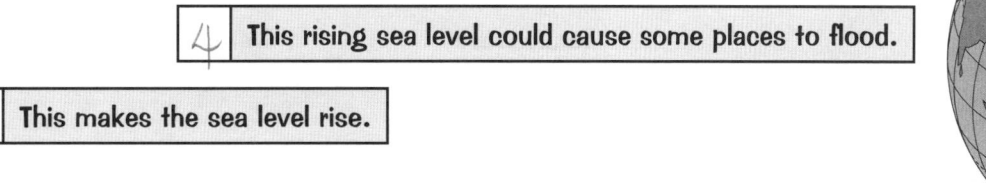

Q4 Complete the sentences by circling the right words.

a) As it gets warmer some places will get less rain. This could cause a **flood** / **(drought)**.

b) Changes in the weather might make it harder to grow **food crops** / **beards**.

c) Some places could get more **droughts** / **(hurricanes)**, which could cause flooding.

Module P2 — Radiation and Life

Electromagnetic Waves and Communication

Q1 a) Circle the right word in the sentence below.

Information can be mixed onto electromagnetic waves to make a **signal** / **picture**.

b) Draw lines to match each type of radiation to the thing that it's used for.

radio waves   satellite TV

microwaves   optical fibres

infrared   normal TV

Q2 a) Are these sentences **true** or **false**? Tick the boxes.

	True	False
Optical fibres are cables with a glass core in the middle.	☐	☐
Optical fibres can carry information.	☐	☐
Optical fibres carry electricity.	☐	☐

b) Which of the following types of radiation can be used in optical fibres? Circle **two** answers.

Microwaves   Visible Light   Ultraviolet

Radio waves   Infrared

Q3 Why can radio waves be used to carry information? Tick the answer.

They can pass through mountains. ☐
They don't get absorbed by the atmosphere. ☐
They can power the radios that pick them up. ☐
They can only travel a short way. ☐

Module P2 — Radiation and Life

Analogue and Digital Signals

Q1 Complete the sentences by circling the right words.

a) Analogue signals vary **digitally** / **continuously**.

b) **Analogue** / **digital** signals can have any number.

c) Digital signals can only be 1 or **2** / **0**.

Q2 Fill in the blanks, choosing from the words below.

clearer	digital	computers	bytes

.... signals can carry pictures and sound.

.... can store and use these signals.

The amount of information used to store pictures or sounds

is measured in ....

More information means .... images or sounds.

Q3 Fill in the blanks in the sentences. Choose from the words below each sentence.

a) Digital signals are affected less by .... than analogue signals.

bytes   pulses   noise

b) Digital signals are .... than analogue signals.

clearer   larger   louder

Q4 a) How many values can a digital signal take? Tick the answer.

1 ☐   2 ☐   3 ☐   4 ☐

b) Look at this signal:

The signal can be written as numbers. Which of these is the signal? Circle the answer.

0101   2221   0000

Module P2 — Radiation and Life

Mixed Questions — Module P2

Q1 a) Draw lines to put the types of electromagnetic radiation in order of **frequency**. One has been done for you.

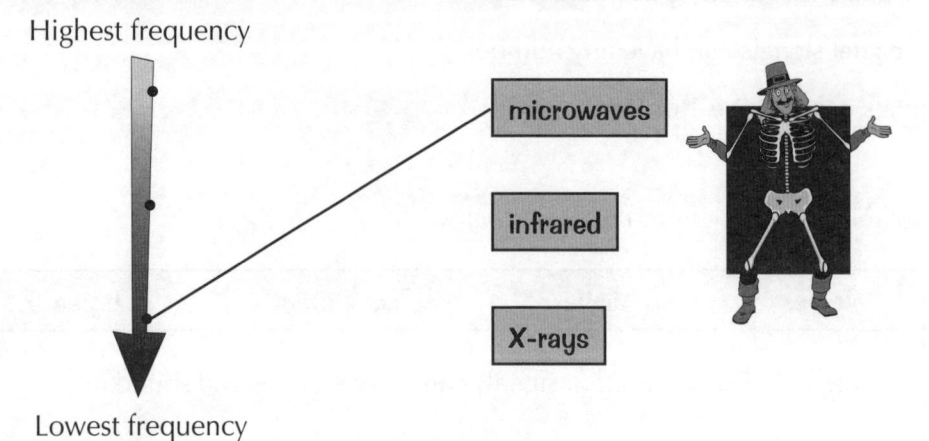

Highest frequency

microwaves

infrared

X-rays

Lowest frequency

b) Draw lines to match the type of radiation with what it's used for.

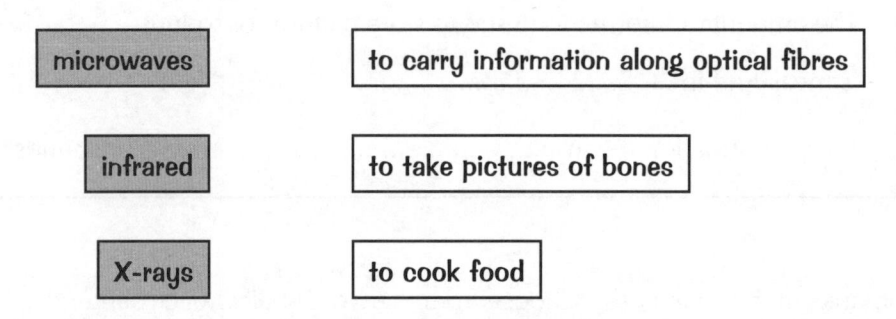

microwaves — to carry information along optical fibres

infrared — to take pictures of bones

X-rays — to cook food

Q2 a) How is carbon dioxide added to the atmosphere? Circle **two** answers.

respiration   eating vegetables   photosynthesis   burning trees   painting trees

b) How is carbon dioxide removed from the atmosphere? Circle **one** answer.

respiration   eating vegetables   photosynthesis   burning trees   painting trees

c) Carbon dioxide is a type of greenhouse gas. Name **two** other greenhouse gases.

1. ....

2. ....

d) The amount of carbon dioxide in the atmosphere is increasing. What is this causing? Tick the box.

☐ Global cooling

☐ Global warming

Module P2 — Radiation and Life

Mixed Questions — Module P2

Q3 a) How are **ions** made? Tick the answer.

☐ Photons with really high energies hit an atom or molecule. This knocks off an electron.

☐ Electrons with really high energies hit an atom or molecule. This knocks off a proton.

☐ Electrons with really low energies hit an atom or molecule. This knocks off a neutron.

b) Ultraviolet radiation is a type of **ionising radiation**. Name **two** other types.

1. ....

2. ....

c) Ultraviolet radiation is absorbed by a layer of the atmosphere. What is this layer called? Tick the box.

☐ Ultraviolet layer   ☐ Ozone layer

Q4 a) How do **microwaves** heat up food? Tick the answer.

☐ Water molecules in food reflect the microwaves.

☐ Water molecules in food absorb the microwaves.

b) Which of the following sentences is **true**? Circle one answer.

A — Microwaves are used to carry information along optical fibres.

B — Microwaves are used in night vision cameras.

C — Microwaves are used to carry mobile phone signals.

c) Which of these sentences is true? Tick one box.

Microwaves carry energy. ☐

Microwave energy is carried by electrons. ☐

Microwaves have the same frequency as gamma rays. ☐

Module P2 — Radiation and Life

Module P3 — Sustainable Energy

Electrical Energy

Q1 Fill in the blanks to complete the sentences.
Choose a word from those listed below each sentence.

a) Current is the movement of .... around a circuit.

        electricity   wires   light

b) The .... of an appliance is how much energy it transfers each second.

  joules   power   efficiency

c) Power is measured in ....

      watts   joules   amps

Q2 Look at the appliances below.

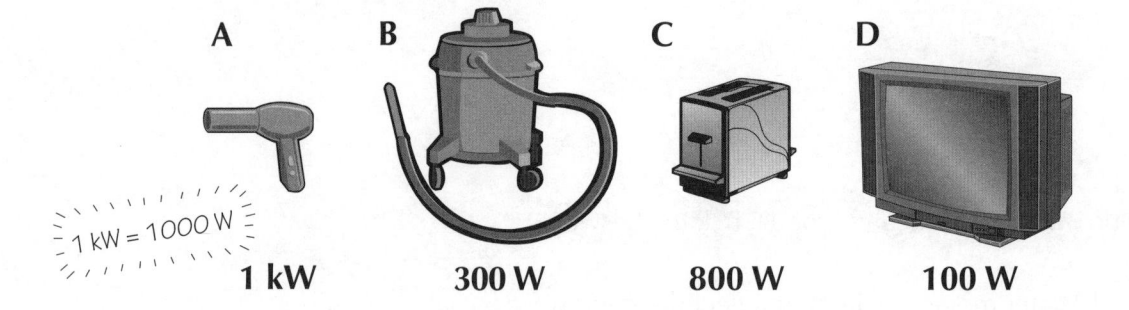

   A   B   C   D

1 kW = 1000 W

  1 kW   300 W   800 W   100 W

a) Which appliance (A–D) transfers the **most** energy per second? ....

b) Which appliance (A–D) transfers the **least** energy per second? ....

Q3 Ed has written some notes about an appliance. However, the paper got torn.

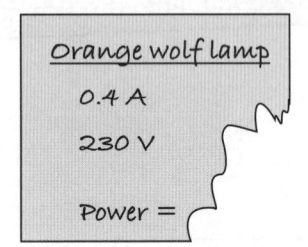

Orange wolf lamp
0.4 A
230 V
Power =

a) What is the voltage of the appliance?

....

b) What is the current through the appliance?

....

c) What is the power of the appliance?   *Power = voltage × current*

....W

Module P3 — Sustainable Energy

Electrical Energy

Q4 Which units do **electricity meters** use to measure the energy you use? Circle the answer.

joules   kilowatt hours   pence

Q5 A washing machine has a power rating of 1.8 kW. It's on for 2 hours. How much energy is transferred? Circle the answer.

Energy transferred (kWh) = Power (kW) × Time (h)

3.8 kWh   0.9 kWh   3.6 kWh   1.1 kWh

Q6 Calculate the **energy** transferred by the following appliances. One has been done for you.

Energy transferred (J) = Power (W) × Time (s)

A **100 watt** lamp in **10 seconds**:
Energy transferred = Power × Time
Energy transferred = 100 W × 10 s = 1000 J

a) A **500 watt** motor in **120 seconds**:
.... J

b) A **1000 watt** heater in **20 seconds**:
.... J

Q7 A water boiler takes **0.5 hours** to boil and has a power of **2.2 kW**. Calculate the **energy** transferred.

Energy transferred (kWh) = Power (kW) × Time (h)

.... kWh

Module P3 — Sustainable Energy

Electrical Energy

Q8 An electric patio heater has a power rating of 2.5 kW. Glenn uses it for 30 minutes.

Divide the number of minutes by 60 to get hours.

a) How many hours is 30 minutes?

....hours

b) How much energy is transferred by the patio heater? Circle the answer.

| 0.2 kWh | 1.25 kWh | 4 kWh | 5 kWh |

Energy transferred (kWh) = Power (kW) × Time (h)

Q9 An oven uses **1.5 kWh** per day. 1 kWh costs **11p**.

Cost = Number of kWh × Cost per kWh

a) Calculate the cost of the energy for the oven per day.

....p

b) The cost of electricity goes up to **12p**.

Calculate the new cost of the energy for the oven per day.

....p

Q10 Boris puts his **2 kW** electric heater on for 3 hours.

a) How many **kilowatt-hours** of electrical energy does the heater use?

.... kWh

b) Electricity costs **7p** per kilowatt-hour.
How much does it cost Boris to use the heater?

....p

Q11 Mr Havel gets his **electricity bill**.
It says he has used **251 kWh** of energy.

1 kWh costs **9p**. How much is Mr Havel's electricity bill?

....p

Module P3 — Sustainable Energy

Efficiency

Q1 Fill in the blank spaces using the words in the box.

light	efficiency	wasted

A lamp transfers electrical energy into useful .... energy.

Some of the electrical energy is .... as heat energy.

The .... of the lamp is the amount of useful energy divided by the total energy supplied.

Q2 Here is an **energy flow diagram** for an electric lamp. Complete the sentences.

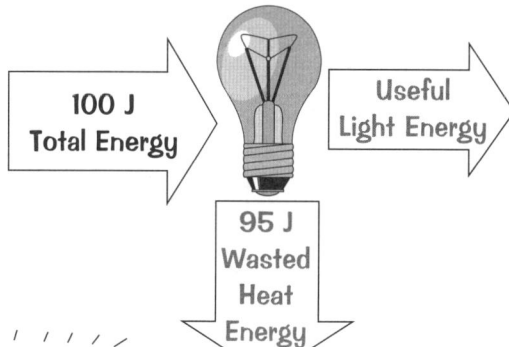

a) The **total energy supplied** is .... J

b) The **energy wasted** is .... J

c) How much energy is **useful**? Circle the answer.

   95 J   5 J   90 J

useful energy = total energy − wasted energy

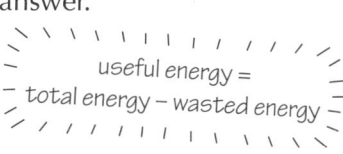

(100 J Total Energy → lamp → Useful Light Energy; 95 J Wasted Heat Energy)

Q3 Calculate how much **useful energy** is given out for each appliance below.

a) 2000 J Total Energy → kettle → Useful Heat Energy; 300 J Wasted Sound and Heat Energy

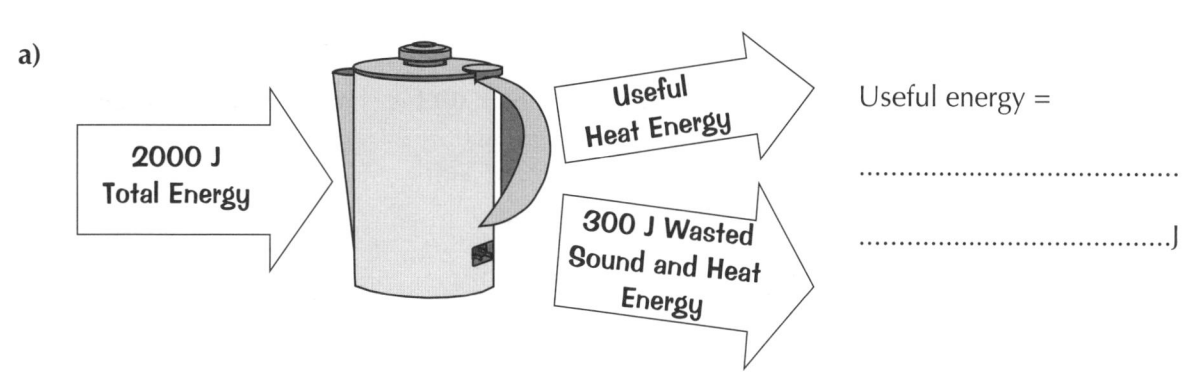

Useful energy =

....

.... J

b) 1000 J Total Energy → hairdryer → Useful Movement and Heat Energy; 100 J Wasted Sound Energy

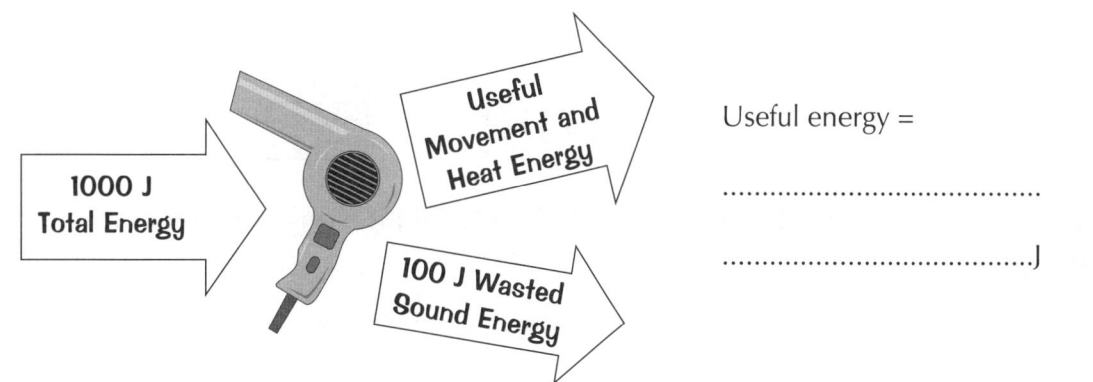

Useful energy =

....

.... J

Module P3 — Sustainable Energy

Efficiency

Example: The total energy into a washing machine is **10 000 J**. The useful energy out is **2000 J**. Calculate its **efficiency**.

Write out the equation for efficiency. → **Efficiency = Useful energy ÷ Total energy**

Efficiency = 2000 ÷ 10 000 = 0.2

Plug the numbers in. Work out the answer with a calculator. Multiply by 100 to get the answer as a percentage (%).

Q4 a) Fill in the **blanks** in the table. Give the efficiency as a decimal.

Efficiency = useful energy ÷ total energy

Appliance	Total Energy (J)	Useful Energy (J)	Wasted Energy (J)	Efficiency
A	2000	1000	1000	1000 ÷ 2000 = 0.5
B	20 000	2 000	18 000	2000 ÷ 20 000 = ...
C	10 000	10 000 – 7000 = ...	7000	.... ÷ 10 000 = ...

b) Which is the **most efficient** appliance in the table? Circle the letter.

Q5 a) A vacuum cleaner uses a **total** energy of **5000 J**. Only **3500 J** is changed to **useful** energy. Calculate its **efficiency**. Give your answer as a percentage.

$$\text{Efficiency} = \frac{\text{useful energy}}{\text{total energy}} \times 100$$

$$= \frac{3500}{5000} \times 100 = \text{.........................} \%$$

b) An electric toothbrush uses a **total** energy of **500 J**. Only **400 J** is changed to **useful** energy. Calculate its **efficiency**. Circle the answer.

80 %   100 %   20 %

c) An electric drill uses a **total** energy of **4000 J**. Only **3000 J** is changed to **useful** energy. Calculate its efficiency. Give your answer as a percentage.

....

.... %

Module P3 — Sustainable Energy

Sankey Diagrams

Q1 a) What does a **Sankey diagram** show? Tick the answer.

| How much of the energy that goes into an appliance is turned into useful energy and how much is wasted. ☐ | How energy is used up by an appliance. ☐ | How the temperature of an appliance changes as it uses energy. ☐ |

b) Circle the correct word to complete the sentence.

The thicker the arrow on a Sankey diagram, the more **energy** / **efficiency** there is.

Q2 Look at the **Sankey diagram** for a blender.

How is **most** of the energy **wasted**? Circle the answer.

as electrical energy   as heat

as kinetic energy   as noise

1000 J electrical energy in

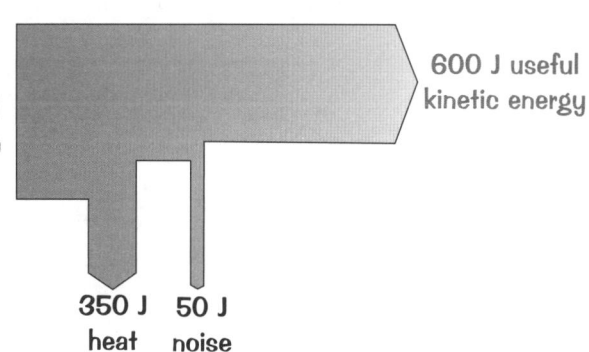

600 J useful kinetic energy

350 J heat   50 J noise

Q3 Look at the Sankey diagram for a **power station**.

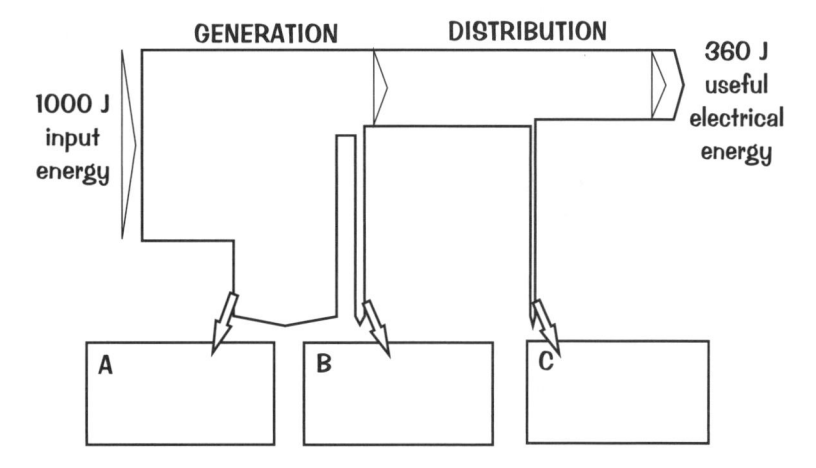

GENERATION   DISTRIBUTION

1000 J input energy

360 J useful electrical energy

A   B   C

a) The labels A, B and C show wasted energy. Fill in the missing labels using those shown below.

80 J noise energy   520 J heat energy   40 J heat energy in wires

b) Calculate the **efficiency** of the power station. Write your answer as a decimal.

Efficiency = useful energy ÷ total energy

....

....

Module P3 — Sustainable Energy

Saving Energy

Q1 Circle the correct word in each sentence.

a) As the population grows, **more** / **less** energy is needed.

b) Some **energy** / **light** sources may eventually run out.

c) Using lots of energy can be bad for the **National Grid** / **environment**.

d) People should try to **reduce** / **increase** the amount of energy they use.

Q2 How can people **save energy** in their homes? Tick **three** answers.

Leave appliances on when they're not being used. ☐

Use more efficient appliances. ☐

Turn the heating down. ☐

Try to stop heat from escaping. ☐

Leave doors and windows open as often as possible. ☐

Q3 A **hot water tank jacket** and **loft insulation** can save money on heating bills.

	Hot water tank jacket	Loft insulation
Cost	£60	£200
Amount Saved Per Year	£15	£100
Time To Pay For Itself	£60 ÷ £15 = 4 years	....

a) Calculate the time **loft insulation** takes to pay for itself. Write your answer in the table above.

time to pay for itself = cost ÷ amount saved per year

b) Which takes the **least** amount of **time to pay for itself**? Circle the answer.

hot water tank jacket   loft insulation

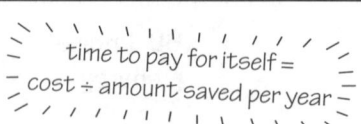

Module P3 — Sustainable Energy

Energy Sources and Power Stations

Q1 Complete the sentences.
Choose the correct word from below each sentence.

a) Electricity is a .... energy source.
   primary   secondary

b) Coal-fired power stations are .... power stations.
   thermal   nuclear

c) Thermal power stations produce ....
   coal   heat

d) Electricity .... be transmitted over long distances.
   can   can't

Q2 Are the sentences **true** or **false**? Tick the boxes.

		True	False
a)	Fossil fuels are a renewable energy source.	☐	☐
b)	Burning fossil fuels produces no carbon dioxide.	☐	☐
c)	Carbon dioxide can lead to climate change.	☐	☐
d)	Burning fossil fuels has no effect on climate change.	☐	☐

Q3 a) Use the words in the box to fill in the gaps.

turbine	generator	steam	water

In a thermal power station, primary energy sources are used to

heat ....

This process produces ....

Steam is used to turn a ....

The movement is converted into electricity by a ....

b) Circle the correct word.

Many **renewable** / **non-renewable** energy sources drive a turbine **without steam**.

Module P3 — Sustainable Energy

Nuclear Energy

Q1 Below is a block diagram of a nuclear power station. Circle the correct word in each section.

| Nuclear fuel releases lots of **heat / kinetic** energy. | → | The energy **cools / heats** water to make steam. | → | The steam turns a **turbine / turnstile**. | → | This drives a **generator / thermostat** which makes electricity. |

Q2 a) Which sentence is an **advantage** of nuclear power? Tick **one** answer.

Nuclear power stations cost a lot to build. ☐

Nuclear power stations don't produce carbon dioxide. ☐

Nuclear power stations produce radioactive waste. ☐

b) Is nuclear fuel a **renewable** or **non-renewable** energy source? ....

Q3 Circle the correct word(s) in the sentences.

The main pollution from a nuclear power station is **radioactive waste / carbon dioxide**.

This pollution gives off **infrared / ionising** radiation.

Exposure to this radiation can cause damage to **electrical devices / living cells**.

Lots of exposure to this radiation can lead to **cancer / heart disease**.

Q4 a) Draw lines to join up each word with its meaning.

Contamination — Being exposed to radiation without having contact with the source.

Irradiation — Picking up a radioactive source that's giving off radiation.

b) Charlie drank water from a river with radioactive waste in it.

Is this an example of **irradiation** or **contamination**?

....

Module P3 — Sustainable Energy

Wind and Solar Energy

Q1 Complete the sentence. Choose from the words given.

> Solar cells make electricity from ....

water   sunlight   wind

Q2 Are the sentences are **true** or **false**? Tick the boxes.

		True	False
a)	The noise from wind turbines might annoy people living near them.	☐	☐
b)	Wind turbines produce lots of carbon dioxide.	☐	☐
c)	Some people think wind turbines spoil the view of the landscape.	☐	☐
d)	Wind power has high running costs.	☐	☐

Q3 Which of these sentences are **advantages** of solar cells? Tick **three** boxes.

- ☐ They don't produce any polluting waste.
- ☐ They don't work when it isn't very windy.
- ☐ They don't need fuel.
- ☐ They have low running costs.
- ☐ They need lots of power cables.

Q4 Do the sentences describe **wind power**, **solar power** or **both**? Tick the boxes.

	Wind Power	Solar Power	Both
The energy source is renewable.			
The start up costs are high.			
Energy is only produced when it's sunny.			
No carbon dioxide is produced when using the energy source.			
It can be very noisy.			
Most energy is produced when it's very windy.			

Module P3 — Sustainable Energy

Wave and Tidal Energy

Q1 a) The sentences below explain how electricity is made from **wave power**. Number them 1 to 4 to put them in the **right order**. One has been done for you.

- [ ] The air makes the turbine spin.
- [ ] The generator makes electricity.
- [1] A wave pushes air through a turbine.
- [ ] The turbine drives a generator.

b) Circle the correct word(s) in the sentences.

> Wave power produces **lots of / no** carbon dioxide.
>
> The start up costs of wave power are **high / low**.
>
> Wave power is **non-renewable / renewable**.
>
> Wave power produces **lots of / no** pollution.

Q2 Give **one disadvantage** of **tidal energy**.

....

....

Q3 Which energy source depends below on the **weather**? Circle the answer.

- wave power
- tidal energy

Q4 I use the movement of **water**.
I use the **gravity** of the Sun and Moon.
I use **dams** at the end of a **river**.

Which type of renewable energy am I?

....

Module P3 — Sustainable Energy

Biofuels and Geothermal Energy

Q1 a) Where do biofuels come from?

Tick the answer.

☐ sea water
☐ geothermal energy
☐ plants and rotting waste
☐ rocks underground

b) Some advantages and disadvantages of biofuels are written below. Put them into the table.

Forests are chopped down and burnt to make space to grow them.

They are carbon neutral.

They can be made quickly.

Advantages	Disadvantages

Q2 The diagram shows how **geothermal energy** is used. Draw lines to match each letter to its label.

A — A generator driven by the turbine makes electricity.

B — Steam is used to power a turbine.

C — Water is pumped down to hot rocks.

D — The water turns to steam and returns to the surface.

Q3 Are the sentences **true** or **false**? Tick the boxes.

   True   False
a) Geothermal energy causes lots of pollution. ☐ ☐
b) Geothermal energy has high running costs. ☐ ☐
c) Geothermal energy is renewable. ☐ ☐

Module P3 — Sustainable Energy

Hydroelectricity and Reliable Fuel Supplies

Q1 Complete the block diagram about **hydroelectricity**. Use the words from the list.

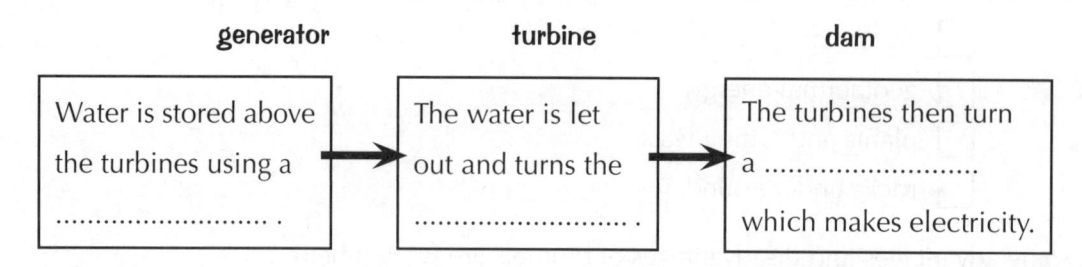

generator   turbine   dam

| Water is stored above the turbines using a .... | → | The water is let out and turns the .... | → | The turbines then turn a .... which makes electricity. |

Q2 Wendy and George are talking about the UK's energy sources. Only one of them is **right**.

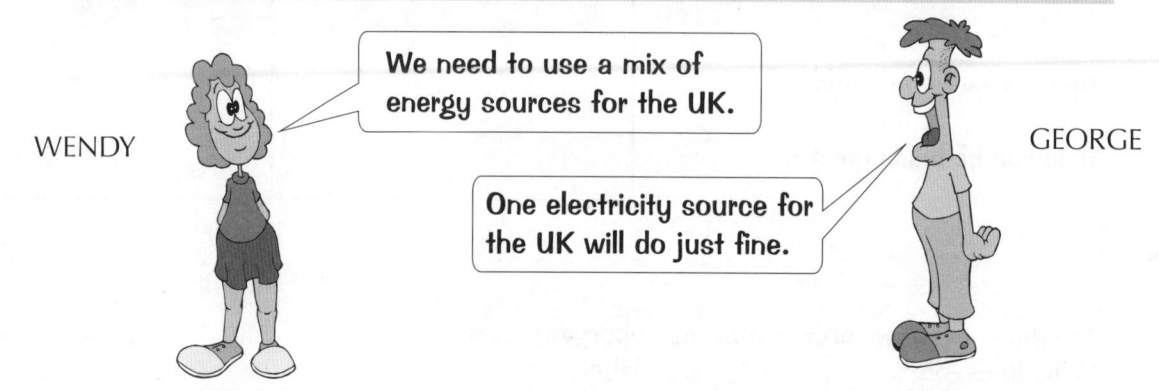

WENDY: "We need to use a mix of energy sources for the UK."

GEORGE: "One electricity source for the UK will do just fine."

a) Who is **right**, Wendy or George? ....

b) Explain your answer to part **a**).

....

Q3 a) The sentences below are about **hydroelectricity**. Are the sentences **true** or **false**? Tick the boxes.

	True	False
It produces no carbon dioxide when running.	☐	☐
It has high fuel costs.	☐	☐
It produces a lot of pollution when running.	☐	☐
It has low running costs.	☐	☐

b) Give one **disadvantage** of hydroelectricity.

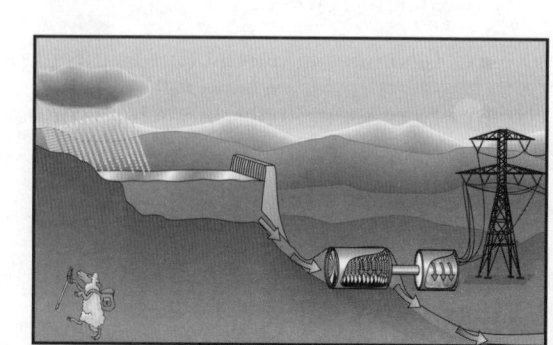

....

....

Module P3 — Sustainable Energy

Comparing Energy Resources

Q1 Look at the data for **wind power** and **nuclear power** in the table. Use the table to answer the questions.

	Wind power	Nuclear power
Running cost per unit of electricity produced	3-4p	4-7p
Efficiency (%)	35	38
Carbon dioxide produced per unit of electricity (g)	0	110

a) Which energy source costs less to run, **wind power** or **nuclear power**?

....

b) Which energy source is more efficient, **wind power** or **nuclear power**?

....

c) Which energy source produces more carbon dioxide, **wind power** or **nuclear power**?

....

Q2 a) Which type of power station is usually the **cheapest** to run? Tick the box.

☐ Renewable energy power stations ☐ Non-renewable energy power stations

b) Why is it cheaper to run this type of power station? Circle the answer.

The energy sources used are free.

People can be paid less to work in power stations that use this energy source.

They make more electricity.

Q3 Name the type of power station that makes **radioactive waste**.

....

Module P3 — Sustainable Energy

Generators and the National Grid

Q1 a) How does a **generator** work? Use the words in the box to fill in the blanks.

| electricity | generator | magnet | turbine |

When a .... is turned it moves a magnet.

The magnet is near to a coil of wire in the ....

The spinning .... makes a voltage in the coil of wire.

This voltage creates a flow of ....

b) If a generator produces a bigger current, does it use **more or less** fuel? ....

Q2 Which sentence describes the **National Grid**? Tick the answer.

It's the network of pylons and electrical cables that supply electricity to the whole of Britain. ☐

It's the money spent each year on making Britain's electricity supply better. ☐

It's the biggest power station in Britain. ☐

Q3 Electricity is sent out around the country at a **high voltage**. However, the mains voltage is much **lower**.

a) Why is electricity sent out at a **high voltage**?

....

b) What voltage is the UK **mains supply**?

.... volts

Module P3 — Sustainable Energy

Mixed Questions — Module P3

Q1 Put the energy sources in the table to show if they're **renewable** or **non-renewable**. One has been done for you.

nuclear fuel wind oil biofuel waves ~~coal~~

Renewable	Non-renewable
	coal

Q2 The diagram shows how electricity is made in a thermal power station. Fill in the blank labels using the words in the list.

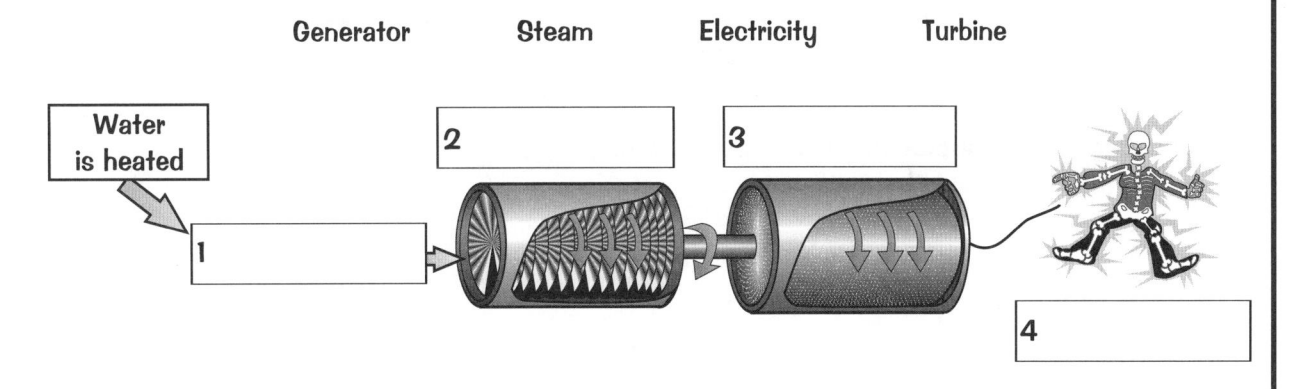

Generator   Steam   Electricity   Turbine

Water is heated

1

2

3

4

Q3 a) Give one **advantage** of **nuclear power**.

....

....

b) Which of these produces ionising radiation? Circle the answer.

Radioactive waste from nuclear power stations.

The waste from using biofuels.

The pollution caused by fossil fuel power stations.

Module P3 — Sustainable Energy

Mixed Questions — Module P3

Q4 An electric sander is used for **0.5 hours**. It has a power of **0.3 kW**.

Energy transferred (kWh) = Power (kW) × Time (h)

a) Calculate how much energy is transferred by the sander.

....

.... kWh

b) Electricity costs **20p per kWh**.
Calculate how much it will cost to use the sander for **0.5 hours**.
You will need to use your answer from part a).

Cost = kWh × Cost per kWh

....

.... p

Q5 The table shows information for two appliances.

Appliance	Total Energy (J)	Wasted Energy (J)	Useful energy (J)
A	2200	1100	
B	1500	300	1200

a) Calculate the **useful energy** for appliance **A**.
Write your answer below.

....

.... J

Useful energy = total energy − wasted energy

b) Calculate the **efficiency** of appliance **A**.
Give your answer as a **decimal**.

....

....

....

Efficiency = useful energy ÷ total energy

c) Calculate the **efficiency** of appliance **B**.
Give your answer as a **percentage**.

....

....

.... %

$$\text{Efficiency} = \frac{\text{useful energy}}{\text{total energy}} \times 100$$

Module P3 — Sustainable Energy